2nd Workshop on Computational Linguistics and Writing 2012 (CLW 2012)

Linguistic and Cognitive Aspects of Document Creation and Document Engineering

Held at the 13th Conference of the European Chapter of the Association for Computational Linguistics (EACL 2012)

Avignon, France
23-24 April 2012

ISBN: 978-1-62276-472-3

Printed from e-media with permission by:

Curran Associates, Inc.
57 Morehouse Lane
Red Hook, NY 12571

Some format issues inherent in the e-media version may also appear in this print version.

Printed by Curran Associates, Inc. (2013)

For permission requests, please contact the Association for Computational Linguistics at the address below.

Association for Computational Linguistics
209 N. Eighth Street
Stroudsburg, Pennsylvania 18360

Phone: 1-570-476-8006
Fax: 1-570-476-0860

acl@aclweb.org

Additional copies of this publication are available from:

Curran Associates, Inc.
57 Morehouse Lane
Red Hook, NY 12571 USA
Phone: 845-758-0400
Fax: 845-758-2634
Email: curran@proceedings.com
Web: www.proceedings.com

Introduction

Writing, whether professional, academic, or private, needs editors, input tools and display devices, and involves the coordination of cognitive, linguistic, and technical aspects. Most texts composed in the 21st century are probably created on electronic devices; people compose texts in word processors, text editors, content management systems, blogs, wikis, e-mail clients, and instant messaging applications. Texts are rendered and displayed on very small and very large screens, they are meant to be read by experts and laypersons, and they are supposed to be interactive and printable all at the same time.

The production of documents has been researched from various perspectives:

- Writing research has been concerned with text processing tools and cognitive processes since the 1970s. The current rise of new writing environments and genres (e.g., blogging), as well as new possibilities to observe text production in the workplace, has prompted new studies in this area of research.
- Document engineering is concerned with aspects of rendering and displaying textual and other resources for the creation, maintenance, and management of documents. Writers today use tools for layout design, collaborating with co-authors, and tracking changes in the production process with versioning systems—all of these are active research areas in document engineering.
- Computational linguistics has mostly been concerned with static or finished texts. There is now a growing need to explore how computational linguistics can support human text production and interactive text processing. Methods from natural language processing can also provide support for exploring data relevant for writing research (e.g., keystroke-logging data) and document engineering (e.g., tailoring documents to specific user needs).

CL&W 2010, held at NAACL 2010 in Los Angeles, was a successful workshop, offering researchers from different but related disciplines a platform for sharing findings and ideas. This follow-on Workshop on Computational Linguistics and Writing brings together researchers from the communities listed above to stimulate discussion and cooperation between these areas of research.

We received 9 submissions from both computational linguistics and writing researchers. After a rigorous review process we selected 6 papers for the workshop. We would like to thank the members of the Program Committee or their excellent work—the reviews were all very thorough, carefully written, and detailed, and helped the authors to improve their papers.

The papers included here present research that explores writing processes, text production, and document engineering principles as well as actual working systems that support novice and expert writers in one or more aspects when producing a document. We are pleased to present these papers in this volume.

We hope the work presented at CL&W 2012 will foster discussion and collaboration between researchers, bringing together expertise and interest from different but related fields.

Michael Piotrowski, Cerstin Mahlow, and Robert Dale

Organizers:

Michael Piotrowski, University of Zurich (Switzerland)
Cerstin Mahlow. University of Basel (Switzerland)
Robert Dale, Macquarie University (Australia)

Program Committee:

Gerd Bräuer, University of Education Freiburg (Germany)
Jill Burstein, ETS (USA)
Rickard Domeij, The Language Council of Sweden (Sweden)
Kevin Egan, University of Southern California (USA)
Caroline Hagège, Xerox Research Centre Europe (France)
Sofie Johansson Kokkinakis, University of Gothenburg (Sweden)
Ola Karlsson, The Language Council of Sweden (Sweden)
Ola Knutsson, KTH (Sweden)
Eva Lindgren, Umeå University (Sweden)
Aurélien Max, LIMSI (France)
Guido Nottbusch, University of Bielefeld (Germany)
Martin Reynaert, Tilburg University (The Netherlands)
Koenraad de Smedt, University of Bergen (Norway)
Sylvana Sofkova Hashemi, University West (Sweden)
Eric Wehrli, University of Geneva (Switzerland)
Carl Whithaus, UC Davis (USA)
Michael Zock, CNRS (France)

Table of Contents

Workshop Program

April 23, 2012

14:00 Opening

Session 1

14:15–14:40 *From character to word level: Enabling the linguistic analyses of Inputlog process data*
Mariëlle Leijten, Lieve Macken, Veronique Hoste, Eric Van Horenbeeck and Luuk Van Waes

14:40–15:05 *From Drafting Guideline to Error Detection: Automating Style Checking for Legislative Texts*
Stefan Höfler and Kyoko Sugisaki

15:05–15:30 *Summary of Research Based on My Reviewers & the Benefits of Aggregated, Crowd-Sourced Assessment*
Joe Moxley

15:30 Coffee Break

Session 2

16:00–16:25 *Google Books N-gram Corpus used as a Grammar Checker*
Rogelio Nazar and Irene Renau

16:25–16:50 *LELIE: a Tool dedicated to Procedure and Requirement Authoring (Demo paper)*
Camille Albert, Flore Barcellini, Corinne Grosse and Patrick Saint-Dizier

16:50–17:15 *Focus Group on Computer Tools Used for Professional Writing and Preliminary Evaluation of LinguisTech*
Marie-Josée Goulet and Annie Duplessis

17:30 Discussion and Closing

From Character to Word Level: Enabling the Linguistic Analyses of Inputlog Process Data

Mariëlle Leijten
Flanders Research Foundation
University of Antwerp
Department of Management
Belgium
marielle.leijten@ua.ac.be

Lieve Macken
LT[3], Language and Translation Technology Team, University College Ghent and Ghent University
Belgium
lieve.macken@hogent.be

Veronique Hoste
LT[3], Language and Translation Technology Team, University College Ghent and Ghent University
Belgium
veronique.hoste@hogent.be

Eric Van Horenbeeck
University of Antwerp
Department of Management
Belgium
eric.vanhorenbeeck@ua.ac.be

Luuk Van Waes
University of Antwerp
Department of Management
Belgium
luuk.vanwaes@ua.ac.be

Abstract

Keystroke-logging tools are widely used in writing process research. These applications are designed to capture each character and mouse movement as isolated events as an indicator of cognitive processes. The current research project explores the possibilities of aggregating the logged process data from the letter level (keystroke) to the word level by merging them with existing lexica and using NLP tools. Linking writing process data to lexica and using NLP tools enables researchers to analyze the data on a higher, more complex level.

In this project the output data of Inputlog are segmented on the sentence level and then tokenized. However, by definition writing process data do not always represent clean and grammatical text. Coping with this problem was one of the main challenges in the current project. Therefore, a parser has been developed that extracts three types of data from the S-notation: word-level revisions, deleted fragments, and the final writing product. The within-word typing errors are identified and excluded from further analyses. At this stage the Inputlog process data are enriched with the following linguistic information: part-of-speech tags, lemmas, chunks, syllable boundaries and word frequencies.

1 Introduction

Keystroke-logging is a popular method in writing research (Sullivan & Lindgren, 2006) to study the underlying cognitive processes (Berninger, 2012). Various keystroke-logging programs have been developed, each with a different focus[1]. The programs differ in the events that are logged

[1] A detailed overview of available keystroke logging programs can be found on http://www.writingpro.eu/logging_programs.php.

Proceedings of the EACL 2012 Workshop on Computational Linguistics and Writing, pages 1–8,
Avignon, France, April 23, 2012.

(keyboard and/or mouse, speech recognition), in the environment that is logged (a program-specific text editor, MS Word or all Windows-based applications), in their combination with other logging tools (e.g., eye tracking and usability tools like Morae) and the analytic detail of the output files. Examples of keystroke-logging tools are:

- Scriptlog: Text editor, Eyetracking (Strömqvist, Holmqvist, Johansson, Karlsson, & Wengelin, 2006),
- Inputlog: Windows environment, speech recognition (Leijten & Van Waes, 2006),
- Translog: Text editor, integration of dictionaries (Jakobsen, 2006) (Wengelin et al., 2009).

Keystroke loggers' data output is mainly based on capturing each character and mouse movement as isolated events. In the current research project[2] we explore the possibilities of aggregating the logged process data from the letter level (keystroke) to the word level by merging them with existing lexica and using NLP tools.

Linking writing process data to lexica and using NLP tools enables us to analyze the data on a higher, more complex level. By doing so we would like to stimulate interdisciplinary research, and relate findings in the domain of writing research to other domains (e.g., Pragmatics, CALL, Translation studies, Psycholinguistics).

We argue that the enriched process data combined with temporal information (time stamps, action times and pauses) will further facilitate the analysis of the logged data and address innovative research questions. For instance, *Is there a developmental shift in the pausing behaviors of writers related to word classes, e.g., before adjectives as opposed to before nouns (cf. cognitive development in language production)? Do translation segments correspond to linguistic units (e.g., comparing speech recognition and keyboarding)? Which linguistic shifts characterize substitutions as a sub type of revisions (e.g., linguistic categories, frequency)?*

A more elaborate example of a research question in which the linguistic information has added value is: *Is the text prodcution of causal markers more cognitive demanding than the production of temporal markers*? In reading research, evidence is found that it takes readers longer to process sentences or paragraphs that contain causal markers than temporal markers. Does the same hold for the production of these linguistic markers? Based on the linguistic information added to the writing process data researchers are now able to easily select causal and temporal markers and compare the process data from various perspectives *(cf. step 4 - linguistic analyses)*.

The work described in this paper is based on the output of Inputlog[3], but it can also be applied to the output of other keystroke-logging programs. To promote more linguistically-oriented writing process research, Inputlog aggregates the logged process data from the character level (keystroke) to the word level. In a subsequent step, we use various Natural Language Processing (NLP) tools to further annotate the logged process data with different kinds of linguistic information: part-of-speech tags, lemmata, chunk boundaries, syllable boundaries, and word frequency.

The remainder of this paper is structured as follows. Section 2 describes the output of Inputlog, and section 3 describes an intermediate level of analysis. Section 4 describes the flow of the linguistic analyses and the various linguistic annotations. Section 5 wraps up with some concluding remarks and suggestions for future research.

2 Inputlog

Inputlog is a word-processor independent keystroke-logging program that not only registers keystrokes, mouse movements, clicks and pauses in MS Word, but also in any other Windows-based software applications.

Keystroke-logging programs store the complete sequence of keyboard and/or mouse events in chronological order. Figure 1 represents "*Volgend jaar*" ('Next Year') at the character and mouse action level.

The keyboard strokes, mouse movements, and mouse clicks are represented in a readable output for each action (e.g., 'SPACE' refers to the spacebar, LEFT Click is a left mouse click, and 'Movement' is a synthesized representation of a continuous mouse movement). Additionally, timestamps indicate when keys are pressed and released, and when mouse movements are made. For each keystroke in MSWord the position of

[2] FWO-Merging writing process data with lexica - 2009-2012

[3] http://www.inputlog.net/

the character in the document is represented as well as the total length of the document at that specific moment. This enables researchers to take the non-linearity of the writing process into account, which is the result of the execution of revisions during the text production.

Event Type	Output	Position	Doclength	StartTime	EndTime	ActionTime	PauseTime
focus	Twitter3.docm - Microsoft Word			3604	3604	0	3604
mouse	LEFT Click			6428	6677	249	6428
mouse	Movement			9594	10577	983	2917
mouse	Movement			23244	24024	780	12667
mouse	LEFT Click			24118	24212	94	94
mouse	Movement			24134	24134	0	0
mouse	Movement			24258	24290	32	124
keyboard	V	0	0	26864	26973	375	2574
keyboard	o	1	1	27160	27238	78	296
keyboard	l	2	2	27363	27534	171	203
keyboard	g	3	3	27456	27581	125	93
keyboard	e	4	4	27534	27706	172	78
keyboard	n	5	5	27675	27784	109	141
keyboard	d	6	6	27862	28018	156	187
keyboard	SPACE	7	7	27987	28127	140	125
keyboard	j	8	8	28127	28268	141	140
keyboard	a	9	9	28268	28330	62	141
keyboard	a	10	10	28408	28517	109	140
keyboard	r	11	11	28486	28658	172	78
keyboard	SPACE	12	12	28611	28736	125	125
keyboard	o	13	13	28689	28829	140	78

Figure 1 Example of general analysis Inputlog.

To represent the non-linearity of the writing process the S-notation is used. The S-notation (Kollberg & Severinson Eklundh, 2002) contains information about the revision types (insertion or deletion), the order of the revisions and the place in the text where the writing process was interrupted. The S-notation can be automatically generated from the keystroke-logging data and has become a standard in the representation of the non-linearity in writing processes.

Figure 2 shows an example of the S-notation. The text is taken from an experiment with master students Multilingual Professional Communication who were asked to write a (Dutch) tweet about a conference (VWEC). The S-notation shows the final product and the process needed.

Volgend·jaar·organiseert·{#$|_4$}^{3}VWEC·een·{boeiend·$|_9$}^{8}con
gres·[over·']$^1|_1$[met·als·thema$|_{10}$]^9{over}^{10}·'Corporate·Comm
unication{'$|_8$}^{7}.[.]$^2|_2$[·Wat·levert·het·op?'.$|_7$]^6·Blijf·[ons·volge
n·op$|_5$]^4{op·de·hoogte·via$|_6$}^{5}·www.vwec2012.be.$|_3$·

Figure 2. Example of S-notation.

The following conventions are used in S-notation:

- $|_i$: a break in the writing process with sequential number *i*;
- {insertion}$_i$: an insertion occurring after break *i*;
- [deletion]$_i$: a deletion occurring after break *i*.

The example in Figure 2 can be read as follows:

The writer formulates in one segment "*Volgend jaar organiseert VWEC een congres over*" (*'*Next year VWEC organises a conference on*')*. She decides to delete "*over*" (index 1) and then adds the remainder of her first draft "*met als thema 'Corporate Communication. Wat levert het op'?.*" (*'*themed 'Corporate Communication. What is in it for us'?.*')* She deletes a full stop and ends with "*Blijf ons volgen op www.vwec2012.be.*" (*'*Follow us on www.vwec2012.be*')*. The third revision is the addition of the hashtag before VWEC. Then she rephrases "*ons volgen op*" into "*op de hoogte via.*" She notices that her tweet is too long (max. 140 characters) and she decides to delete the subtitle of the conference. She adds the adjective "*boeiend*" ('interesting') to conference and ends by deleting "*met als thema*" ('themed*'*).

3 Intermediate level

At the intermediate level, Inputlog data can also be used to analyze data at the digraph level, for instance, to study interkey intervals (or digraph latency) in relation to typing speed, keyboard efficiency of touch typists and others, dyslexia and keyboard fluency, biometric verification etc. For this type of research, logging data can be leveled up to an intermediate level in which two consecutive events are treated as a unit (e.g., un-ni-it).

Grabowski's research on the internal structure of students' keyboard skills in different writing tasks is a case in point (Grabowski, 2008). He studied whether there are patterns of overall keyboard behavior and whether such patterns are stable across different (copying) tasks. Across tasks, typing speed turned out to be the most stable characteristic of a keyboard user. Another example is the work by Nottbush and his colleagues. Focusing on linguistic aspects of interkey intervals, their research (Nottbusch, 2010; Sahel, Nottbusch, Grimm, & Weingarten, 2008) shows that the syllable boundaries within words have an effect on the temporal keystroke succession. Syllable boundaries lead to increased interkey intervals at the digraph level.

In recent research Inputlog data has also been used to analyze typing errors at this level (Van Waes & Leijten, 2010). As will be demonstrated in the next section, typing errors complicate the analysis of logging data at the word and sentence level because the linear reconstruction is disrupted. For this purpose a large experimental corpus based on a controlled copying task was analyzed, focusing on five digraphs with different characteristics (frequency, keyboard distribution, left-right coordination). The results of a multilevel analysis show that there is no correlation between the frequency of a digraph and the chance that a typing error occurs. However, typing errors show a limited variation: pressing the adjacent key explains more than 40% of the errors, both for touch typists and others; the chance that a typing error is made is related to the characteristics of the digraph, and the individual typing style. Moreover, the median pausing time preceding a typing error tends to be longer than the median interkey transitions of the intended digraph typed correctly. These results illustrate that further research should make it possible to identify and isolate typing errors in logged process data and build an algorithm to filter them during data preparation. This would benefit parsing at a later stage (see section 4).

4 Flow of linguistic analyses

As explained above, writing process data gathered via the traditional keystroke-logging tools are represented at the *character level* and produce *non-linear data* (containing sentence fragments, unfinished sentences/words and spelling errors). These two characteristics are the main obstacles that we need to cope with to analyze writing process data on a higher level. In this section we explain the flow of the linguistic analyses.

4.1 Step 1 - aggregate letter to word level

Natural Language Processing tools, such as part-of-speech taggers, lemmatizers and chunkers are trained on (completed) sentences and words. Therefore, to use the standard NLP tools to enrich the process data with linguistic information, in a first step, words, word groups, and sentences are extracted from the process data.

The S-notation was used as a basis to further segment the data into sentences and tokenize them. A dedicated sentence segmenting and tokenizer module was developed to conduct this process. This dedicated module can cope with the specific S-notation annotations such as insertion, deletion and break markers.

4.2 Step 2 – parsing the S-notation

As mentioned before, standard NLP tools are designed to work with clean, grammatically correct text. We thus decided to treat word-level revisions differently than higher-level revisions and to distinguish deleted fragments from the final writing product.

We developed a parser that extracts three types of data from the S-notation: word-level revisions, deleted fragments, and the final writing product. The word-level revisions can be extracted from the S-notation by retaining all words with word-internal square or curly brackets (see excerpt 1).

(1 - word level revision)

Delet[r]ion incorrect: Deletrion; correct: deletion
In{s}ertion incorrect: Inertion; correct: insertion

Conceptually, the deleted fragments can be extracted from the S-notation by retaining only the words and phrases that are surrounded by word-external square brackets (2); and the final product data can be obtained by deleting everything in between square brackets from the S-notation. In practice, the situation is more complicated as insertions and deletions can be nested.

An example of the three different data types extracted from the S-notation is presented in the excerpt below. To facilitate the readability of the resulting data, the indices are omitted (3).

(2 - deleted fragments)

Volgend·jaar·organiseert·{#}VWEC·een·{boeiend·}co
ngres·[over·'][met·als·thema]{over}·'Corporate·Comm
unication{'}.[.][·Wat·levert·het·op?'.]·Blijf·[ons·volgen
·op]{op·de·hoogte·via|}·www.vwec2012.be.|·

(3 - final writing product)

Volgend·jaar·organiseert·{#}VWEC·een·{boeiend·}co
ngres·[over·'][met·als·thema]{over}·'Corporate·Comm
unication{'}.[.][·Wat·levert·het·op?'.]·Blijf·[ons·volgen
·op]{op·de·hoogte·via|}·www.vwec2012.be.|·

English translation
Next year #VWEC organises an interesting conference about Corporate Communication. Follow us on www.vwec2012.be

In sum, the output of Inputlog data is segmented in sentences and tokenized. The S-notation is divided into three types of revisions and the within-word typing errors are excluded from further analyses.

Although the set-up of the Inputlog extension is largely language-independent, the NLP tools used are language-dependent. As proof-of-concept, we provide evidence from English and Dutch (See Figure 3).

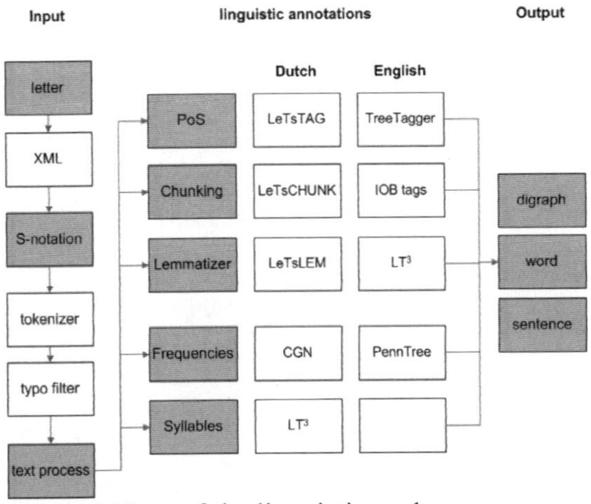

Figure 3 Flow of the linguistic analyses.

4.3 Step 3 – enriching process data with linguistic information

As standard NLP tools are trained on clean data, these tools are not suited for processing input containing spelling errors. Therefore, we only enrich *the final product data* and the *deleted fragments* with different kinds of linguistic annotations. As part-of-speech taggers typically use the surrounding local context to determine the proper part-of-speech tag for a given word (typically a window of two to three words and/or tags is used), the deletions in context are extracted from the S-notation to be processed by the part-of-speech tagger. The deleted fragments in context consist of the whole text string without the insertions and are only used to optimize the results of the linguistic annotation.

(4 - deleted fragments in context)

Volgend·jaar·organiseert·{#}VWEC·een·{boeiend·}co ngres·[over·'][met·als·thema]{over}·'Corporate·Comm unication{'}.[.][·Wat·levert·het·op?'.]·Blijf·[ons·volgen ·op]{op·de·hoogte·via|}·www.vwec2012.be.|·

For the shallow linguistic analysis, we used the LT^3 shallow parsing tools suite consisting of:

- a part-of-speech tagger (LeTsTAG),
- a lemmatizer (LeTsLEMM), and
- a chunker (LeTsCHUNK).

The LT3 tools are platform-independent and hence run on Windows.

Part of speech tags

The English PoS tagger uses the Penn Treebank tag set, which contains 45 distinct tags. The Dutch part-of-speech tagger uses the CGN tag set codes (Van Eynde, Zavrel, & Daelemans, 2000), which is characterized by a high level of granularity. Apart from the word class, the CGN tag set codes a wide range of morpho-syntactic features as attributes to the word class. In total, 316 distinct tags are discerned.

Lemmata

During lemmatization, for each orthographic token, the base form (lemma) is generated. For verbs, the base form is the infinitive; for most other words, this base form is the stem, i.e., the word form without inflectional affixes. The lemmatizers make use of the predicted PoS codes to disambiguate ambiguous word forms, e.g., Dutch "*landen*" can be an infinitive (base form "*landen*") or plural form of a noun (base form "*land*"). The lemmatizers were trained on the English and Dutch parts of the Celex lexical database respectively (Baayen, Piepenbrock, & van Rijn, 1993).

Chunks

During text chunking syntactically related consecutive words are combined into non-overlapping, non-recursive chunks on the basis of a fairly superficial analysis. The chunks are represented by means of IOB-tags.

In the IOB-tagging scheme, each token belongs to one of the following three types: I (inside), O (outside) and B (begin); the B- en I-tags are followed by the chunk type, e.g., B-VP, I-VP. We adapted the IOB-tagging scheme and added end tag (E) to explicitly mark the end of a chunk. Accuracy sores of part-of-speech taggers and lemmatizers typically fluctuate around 97% to 98%; accuracy scores of 95% to 96% are obtained for chunking.

After annotation, the final writing product, deleted fragments, and word-level corrections are aligned and the indices are restored. Figures 4 and 5 show how we enriched the logged process data with different kinds of linguistic information: lemmata, part-of-speech tags, and chunk boundaries.

We further added some word-level annotations on the final writing product and the deletions,

# revisions	index (begin revision)	index (end revisions)	product	word level corrections	lemma	PoS	Chunk	Syllables	Absolute freq
			Volgend		volgend	ADJ	B-NP	vol-gend	44
			jaar		jaar	N-s	E-NP	jaar	200634
			organiseert		organiseren	V-fin	B-VP	or-ga-ni-seert	13803
1	3	3	#VWEC	_3_{#}_3_VWEC	#VWEC	N-prop-s	B-NP	v-wec	/
			een		een	DET	B-NP	een	2150389
1	8	8	_8_{boeiend}_8_		boeiend	ADJ	I-NP	boe-iend	47
			congres		congres	N-s	E-NP	con-gres	2840
	1								
1	9	1							
1		9							
1	10	10	_10_{over}_10_		over	PREP	B-PP	o-ver	146623
			'Corporate		'Corporate	N-prop	I-PP	cor-po-ra-te	37
1	7	7	Communication'	Communication_7_{'}_7_	communication'	N-prop	E-PP	com-mu-ni-ca-t-io	22
			.		.	PCT			/
1	2	2							
	6								
1		6							
			Blijf		blijven	V-fin	B-VP	blijf	58219
	4								
1		4							
	5		_5_{op		op	PREP	B-PP	op	881849
			de		de	DET	I-PP	de	5827958
			hoogte		hoogte	N-s	E-PP	hoog-te	12674
1		5	via}_5_		via	PREP	I-PP	vi-a	32887
			www.vwec2012.be.		www.vwec2012.be.	SYM	E-PP	www-v-wec-be	/

Figure 4 Final writing product and word-level revisions enriched with linguistic information.

viz., syllable boundaries and word frequencies (see last two columns in Figures 4 and 5).

Syllable boundaries:

The syllabification tools were trained on Celex (http://lt3.hogent.be/en/tools/timbl-syllabification). Syllabification was approached as a classification task: a large instance base of syllabified data is presented to a classification algorithm, which automatically learns from it the patterns needed to syllabify unseen data. Accuracy scores for syllabification reside in the range of 92% to 95%.

Word Frequency

Frequency lists for Dutch and English were compiled on the basis of Wikipedia pages, which were extracted from the XML dump of the Dutch and English Wikipedia of December 2011. We used the Wikipedia Extractor developed by Medialab[4] to extract the text from the wiki files. The Wikipedia text files were further tokenized and enriched with part-of-speech tags and

product	deletions	lemma	PoS	Chunk	Syllables	Absolute freq
Volgend						
jaar						
organiseert						
#VWEC						
een						
_8_{boeiend}_8_						
congres						
	_1_[over	over	PREP	B-PP	o-ver	146623
	']_1__9_[met	'met	N-s	B-PP	met	706784
	als	als	PREP	I-PP	als	231748
	thema]_9_	thema	N-s	E-PP	the-ma	5022
_10_{over}_10_						
'Corporate						
Communication'						
.						
	_2_[.]_2_	.	PCT			
	_6_[Wat	wat	PRON-int	B-NP	wat	61958
	levert	leveren	V-fin	B-VP	le-vert	15043
	het	het	DET	B-NP	het	2301736
	op?'.]_6_	op?'.	N-s	E-VP	op	881849
Blijf						
	_4_[ons	ons	PRON	B-NP	ons	8779
	volgen	volgen	V-inf	E-VP	vol-gen	66786
	op]_4_	op	PREP	B-PP	op	881849
_5_{op						
de						
hoogte						
via}_5_						
www.vwec2012.be.						

Figure 5 Deleted fragments enriched with linguistic information.

[4] http://medialab.di.unipi.it/wiki/Wikipedia_Extractor

lemmata. The Wikipedia frequency lists can thus group different word forms belonging to one lemma.

The current version of the Dutch frequency list has been compiled on the basis of nearly 100 million tokens coming from 395,673 Wikipedia pages, which is almost half of the Dutch Wikipedia dump of December 2011.

Frequencies are presented as absolute frequencies.

4.4 Step 4 - combining process data with linguistic information

In a final step we combine the process data with the linguistic information. Based on the time information provided by Inputlog, researchers can calculate various measures, e.g., length of a pause within, before and after lemmata, part-of-speech tags, and at chunk boundaries.

As an example Table 1 shows the mean pausing time before and after the adjectives and nouns in the tweet. Of course, this is a very small-scale example, but it shows the possibilities of exploring writing process data from a linguistic perspective.

	mean pause before	mean pause after	mean pause within
ADJ	1880	671	148
NOUN	728	1455	232
B (begin)	1412	1174	164
E (end)	685	1353	148
I (inside)	730	1034	144

Table 1. Example of process data and linguistic information

In this example the mean pausing time before adjectives is twice as long as before nouns. The pausing time after such a segment shows the opposite proportion. Also pauses in the beginning of chunks are more than twice as long as in the middle of a chunk.

5 Future research

In this paper we presented how writing process data can be enriched with linguistic information. The annotated output facilitates the linguistic analysis of the logged data and provides a valuable basis for more linguistically-oriented writing process research. We hope that this perspective will further enrich writing process research.

5.1 Additional annotations and analyses

In a first phase we only focused on English and Dutch, but the method can be easily applied to other languages as well provided that the linguistic tools are available for a Windows platform.

For the moment, the linguistic annotations are limited to part-of-speech tags, lemmata, chunk information, syllabification, and word frequency information, but can be extended, e.g., by n-gram frequencies to capture collocations.

By aggregating the logged process data from the character level (keystroke) to the word level, general statistics (e.g., total number of deleted or inserted words, pause length before nouns preceded by an adjective or not) can be generated easily from the output of Inputlog as well.

5.2 Technical flow of Inputlog & linguistic tools

At this point Inputlog is a standalone program that needs to be installed on the same local machine that is used to produce the texts. This makes sense as long as the heaviest part of the work is the logging of a writing process. However, extending the scope from a character based analysis device to a system that supplements fine-grained production and process information to various NLP tools is a compelling reason to rethink the overall architecture of the software.

It is not feasible to install the necessary linguistic software with its accompanying databases on every device. By decoupling the capturing part from the analytics a research group will have a better view on the use of its hard- and software resources while also allowing to solve potential copyright issues. Inputlog is now pragmatically Windows-based, but with the new architecture any tool on any OS will be capable to exchange data and results. It will be possible to add an NLP module that receives Inputlog data through a communication layer. A workflow procedure then presents the data in order to the different NLP packages and collects the final output. Because all data traffic is done with XML files, cooperation between software with different creeds becomes conceivable. Finally, the module has an administration utility handling the necessary user authentication and permits.

Acknowledgements

This study is partially funded by a research grant of the Flanders Research Foundation (FWO 2009-2012).

References

Baayen, R. H., R. Piepenbrock, & H. van Rijn. (1993). The CELEX lexical database on CD-ROM. Philadelphia, PA: Linguistic Data Consortium.

Baayen, R. H., Piepenbrock, R., & van Rijn, H. (1993). The CELEX lexical database on CD-ROM. Philadelphia, PA: Linguistic Data Consortium.

Berninger, V. (2012). Past, Present, and Future Contributions of Cognitive Writing Research to Cognitive Psychology: Taylor and Francis.

Grabowski, J. (2008). The internal structure of university students' keyboard skills. Journal of Writing Research, 1(1), 27-52.

Jakobsen, A. L. (2006). Translog: Research methods in translation. In K. P. H. Sullivan & E. Lindgren (Eds.), Computer Keystroke Logging and Writing: Methods and Applications (pp. 95-105). Oxford: Elsevier.

Kollberg, P., & Severinson Eklundh, K. (2002). Studying writers' revising patterns with S-notation analysis. In T. Olive & C. M. Levy (Eds.), Contemporary Tools and Techniques for Studying Writing (pp. 89-104). Dordrecht: Kluwer Academic Publishers.

Leijten, M., & Van Waes, L. (2006). Inputlog: New Perspectives on the Logging of On-Line Writing. In K. P. H. Sullivan & E. Lindgren (Eds.), Computer Keystroke Logging and Writing: Methods and Applications (pp. 73-94). Oxford: Elsevier.

Nottbusch, G. (2010). Grammatical planning, execution, and control in written sentence production. Reading and Writing, 23(7), 777-801.

Sahel, S., Nottbusch, G., Grimm, A., & Weingarten, R. (2008). Written production of German compounds: Effects of lexical frequency and semantic transparency. Written Language and Literacy, 11(2), 211-228.

Strömqvist, S., Holmqvist, K., Johansson, V., Karlsson, H., & Wengelin, A. (2006). What keystroke logging can reveal about writing. In K. P. H. Sullivan & E. Lindgren (Eds.), Computer Keystroke Logging and Writing: Methods and Applications (pp. 45-71). Oxford: Elsevier.

Sullivan, K. P. H., & Lindgren, E. (2006). Computer Key-Stroke Logging and Writing. Oxford: Elsevier Science.

Van Eynde, F., Zavrel, J., & Daelemans, W. (2000). Part of Speech Tagging and Lemmatisation for the Spoken Dutch Corpus. Paper presented at the Proceedings of the second International Conference on Language Resources and Evaluation (LREC), Athens, Greece.

Van Waes, L., & Leijten, M. (2010). The dynamics of typing errors in text production. Paper presented at the SIG Writing 2010, 12th International Conference of the Earli Special Interest Group on Writing, Heidelberg.

Wengelin, A., Torrance, M., Holmqvist, K., Simpson, S., Galbraith, D., Johansson, V., & Johansson, R. (2009). Combined eyetracking and keystroke-logging methods for studying cognitive processes in text production. Behavior Research Methods, 41(2), 337-351.

From Drafting Guideline to Error Detection: Automating Style Checking for Legislative Texts

Stefan Höfler
University of Zurich, Institute
of Computational Linguistics
Binzmühlestrasse 14
8050 Zürich, Switzerland
hoefler@cl.uzh.ch

Kyoko Sugisaki
University of Zurich, Institute
of Computational Linguistics
Binzmühlestrasse 14
8050 Zürich, Switzerland
sugisaki@cl.uzh.ch

Abstract

This paper reports on the development of methods for the automated detection of violations of style guidelines for legislative texts, and their implementation in a prototypical tool. To this aim, the approach of error modelling employed in automated style checkers for technical writing is enhanced to meet the requirements of legislative editing. The paper identifies and discusses the two main sets of challenges that have to be tackled in this process: (i) the provision of domain-specific NLP methods for legislative drafts, and (ii) the concretisation of guidelines for legislative drafting so that they can be assessed by machine. The project focuses on German-language legislative drafting in Switzerland.

1 Introduction

This paper reports on work in progress that is aimed at providing domain-specific automated style checking to support German-language legislative editing in the Swiss federal administration. In the federal administration of the Swiss Confederation, drafts of new acts and ordinances go through several editorial cycles. In a majority of cases, they are originally written by civil servants in one of the federal offices concerned, and then reviewed and edited both by legal experts (at the Federal Office of Justice) and language experts (at the Federal Chancellery). While the former ensure that the drafts meet all relevant legal requirements, the latter are concerned with the formal and linguistic quality of the texts. To help this task, the authorities have drawn up style guidelines specifically geared towards Swiss legislative texts (Bundeskanzlei, 2003; Bundesamt für Justiz, 2007).

Style guidelines for laws (and other types of legal texts) may serve three main purposes: (i) improving the understandability of the texts (Lerch, 2004; Wydick, 2005; Mindlin, 2005; Butt and Castle, 2006; Eichhoff-Cyrus and Antos, 2008), (ii) enforcing their consistency with related texts, and (iii) facilitating their translatability into other languages. These aims are shared with writing guidelines developed for controlled languages in the domain of technical documentation (Lehrndorfer, 1996; Reuther, 2003; Muegge, 2007).

The problem is that the manual assessment of draft laws for their compliance with all relevant style guidelines is time-consuming and easily inconsistent due to the number of authors and editors involved in the drafting process. The aim of the work presented in this paper is to facilitate this process by providing methods for a consistent automatic identification of some specific guideline violations.

The remainder of the paper is organised as follows. We first delineate the aim and scope of the project presented in the paper (section 2) and the approach we are pursuing (section 3). In the main part of the paper, we then identify and discuss the two main challenges that have to be tackled: the technical challenge of providing NLP methods for legislative drafts (section 4) and the linguistic challenge of concretising the existing drafting guidelines for legislative texts (section 5).

2 Aim and Scope

The aim of the project to be presented in this paper is to develop methods of automated style checking specifically geared towards legislative editing, and to implement these methods in a prototypical tool (cf. sections 3 and 4). We work towards automat-

Proceedings of the EACL 2012 Workshop on Computational Linguistics and Writing, pages 9–18,
Avignon, France, April 23, 2012.

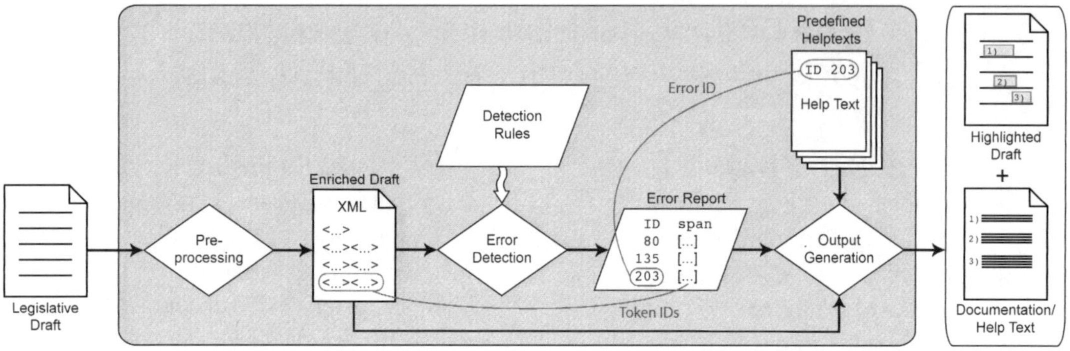

Figure 1: Architecture of the style checking system.

ically detecting violations of existing guidelines, and where these guidelines are very abstract, we concretise them so that they become detectable by machine (cf. section 5). However, it is explicitly not the goal of our project to propose novel style rules.

We have adopted a broad conception of "style checking" that is roughly equivalent to how the term, and its variant "controlled language checking," have been used in the context of technical writing (Geldbach, 2009). It comprises the assessment of various aspects of text composition controlled by specific writing guidelines (typographical conventions, lexical preferences, syntax-related recommendations, constraints on discourse and document structure), but it does not include the evaluation of spelling and grammar.

While our project focuses on style checking for German-language Swiss federal laws (the federal constitution, acts of parliament, ordinances, federal decrees, cantonal constitutions), we believe that the challenges arising from the task are independent of the chosen language and legislative system but pertain to the domain in general.

3 Approach

The most important innovative contribution of our project is the enhancement of the method of error modelling to meet the requirements of legislative editing. Error modelling means that texts are searched for specific features that indicate a style guideline violation: the forms of specific "errors" are thus anticipated and modelled.

The method of error modelling has mainly been developed for automated style checking in the domain of technical writing. Companies often control the language used in their technical documentation in order to improve the understandability, readability and translatability of these texts. Controlled language checkers are tools that evaluate input texts for compliance with such style guidelines set up by a company.[1]

State-of-the-art controlled language checkers work along the following lines. In a pre-processing step, they first perform an automatic analysis of the input text (tokenisation, text segmentation, morphological analysis, part-of-speech tagging, parsing) and enrich it with the respective structural and linguistic information. They then apply a number of pre-defined rules that model potential "errors" (i.e. violations of individual style guidelines) and aim at detecting them in the analysed text. Most checkers give their users the option to choose which rules the input text is to be checked for. Once a violation of the company's style guidelines has been detected, the respective passage is highlighted and an appropriate help text is made available to the user (e.g. as a comment in the original document or in an extra document generated by the system). The system we are working on is constructed along the same lines; its architecture is outlined in Fig. 1.

Transferring the described method to the domain of legislative editing has posed challenges to both pre-processing and error modelling. The peculiarities of legal language and legislative texts have necessitated a range of adaptations in the NLP procedures devised, and the guidelines for legislative drafting have required highly domain-specific

[1]Examples of well-developed commercial tools that offer such style checking for technical texts are acrolinx IQ by Acrolinx and CLAT by IAI.

error modelling, which needed to be backed up by substantial linguistic research. We will detail these two sets of challenges in the following two sections.

4 Pre-Processing

4.1 Tokenisation

The legislative drafters and editors we are targeting exclusively work with MS Word documents. Drafters compose the texts in Word, and legislative editors use the commenting function of Word to add their suggestions and corrections to the texts they receive. We make use of the XML representation (WordML) underlying these documents. In a first step, we tokenise the text contained therein and assign each token an ID directly in the WordML structure. We then extract the text material (including the token IDs and some formatting information that proves useful in the processing steps to follow) for further processing. The token IDs are used again at the end of the style checking process when discovered styleguide violations are highlighted by inserting a Word comment at the respective position in the WordML representation of the original document. The output of our style checker is thus equivalent to how legislative editors make their annotations to the drafts – a fact that proves essential with regard to the tool being accepted by its target users.

4.2 Text Segmentation

After tokenisation, the input text is then segmented into its structural units. Legislative texts exhibit a sophisticated domain-specific structure. Our text segmentation tool detects the boundaries of chapters, sections, articles, paragraphs, sentences and enumeration elements, and marks them by adding corresponding XML tags to the text.

There are three reasons why text segmentation is crucial to our endeavour:

1. Proper text segmentation ensures that only relevant token spans are passed on to further processing routines (e.g. sentences contained in articles must to be passed on to the parser, whereas article numbers or section headings must not).

2. Most structural units are themselves the object of style rules (e.g. "sections should not contain more than twelve articles, articles should not contain more than three paragraphs and paragraphs should not contain more than one sentence"). The successful detection of violations of such rules depends on the correct delimitation of the respective structural units in the text.

3. Certain structural units constitute the context for other style rules (e.g. "the sentence right before the first element of an enumeration has to end in a colon"; "the antecedent of a pronoun must be within the same article"). Here too, correct text segmentation constitutes the prerequisite for an automated assessment of the respective style rules.

We have devised a line-based pattern-matching algorithm with look-around to detect the boundaries of the structural units of legislative drafts (Höfler and Piotrowski, 2011). The algorithm also exploits formatting information extracted together with the text from the Word documents. However, not all formatting information has proven equally reliable: as the Word documents in which the drafts are composed do only make use of style environments to a very limited extent, formatting errors are relatively frequent. Font properties such as italics or bold face, or the use of list environments are frequently erroneous and can thus not be exploited for the purpose of delimiting text segments; headers and newline information, on the other hand, have proven relatively reliable.

Figure 2 illustrates the annotation that our tool yields for the excerpt shown in the following example:

(1) *Art. 14 Amtsenthebung* [2]
Die Wahlbehörde kann eine Richterin oder einen Richter vor Ablauf der Amtsdauer des Amtes entheben, wenn diese oder dieser:

   a. vorsätzlich oder grobfahrlässig Amtspflichten schwer verletzt hat; oder
   b. die Fähigkeit, das Amt auszuüben, auf Dauer verloren hat.

Art. 14 Removal from office
The electoral authorities may remove a judge from office before he or she has completed his or her term where he or she:

[2] Patentgerichtsgesetz (Patent Court Act), SR 173.41; for the convenience of readers, examples are also rendered in the (non-authoritative) English version published at `http://www.admin.ch/ch/e/rs/rs.html`.

```
<article>
   <article_head>
      <article_type>Art.</article_type>
      <article_nr>14</article_nr>
      <article_header>Amtsenthebung</article_header>
   </article_head>
   <article_body>
      <paragraph>
         <sentence>
            Die Wahlbehörde kann eine Richterin oder einen Richter vor Ablauf der Amtsdauer
            des Amtes entheben, wenn diese oder dieser:
               <enumeration>
                  <enumeration_element>
                     <element_nr type="letter">a.</element_nr>
                     <element_text>
                        vorsätzlich oder grobfahrlässig Amtspflichten schwer verletzt hat;
                        oder
                     </element_text>
                  </enumeration_element>
                  <enumeration_element>
                     <element_nr type="letter">b.</element_nr>
                     <element_text>
                        die Fähigkeit, das Amt auszuüben, auf Dauer verloren hat.
                     </element_text>
                  </enumeration_element>
               </enumeration>
            </sentence>
      </paragraph>
   </article_body>
</article>
```

Figure 2: Illustration of the text segmentation provided by the tool. Excerpt: Article 14 of the Patent Court Act. (Token delimiters and any other tags not related to text segmentation have been omitted in the example.)

a. wilfully or through gross negligence commits serious breaches of his or her official duties; or
b. has permanently lost the ability to perform his or her official duties.

As our methods must be robust in the face of input texts that are potentially erroneous, the text segmentation provided by our tool does not amount to a complete document parsing; our text segmentation routine rather performs a document chunking by trying to detect as many structural units as possible.

Another challenge that arises from the fact that the input texts may be erroneous is that features whose absence we later need to mark as an error cannot be exploited for the purpose of detecting the boundaries of the respective contextual unit. A colon, for instance, cannot be used as an indicator for the beginning of an enumeration since we must later be able to search for enumerations that are not preceded by a sentence ending in a colon as this constitutes a violation of the respective style rule. Had the colon been used as an indicator for the detection of enumeration boundaries, only enumerations preceded by a colon would have been marked as such in the first place. The development of adequate pre-processing methods constantly faces such dilemmas. It is thus necessary to always anticipate the specific guideline violations that one later wants to detect on the basis of the information added by any individual pre-processing routine.

Special challenges also arise with regard to the task of sentence boundary detection. Legislative texts contain special syntactic structures that off-the-shelf tools cannot process and that therefore need special treatment. Example (1) showed a sentence that runs throughout a whole enumeration; colon and semicolons do not mark sentence boundaries in this case. To complicate matters even further, parenthetical sentences may be inserted behind individual enumeration items, as shown in example (2).

(2) *Art. 59 Abschirmung* [3]
[1] Der Raum oder Bereich, in dem stationäre Anlagen oder radioaktive Strahlenquellen betrieben oder gelagert werden, ist so zu

[3] Strahlenschutzverordnung (Radiological Protection Ordinance), SR 814.50; emphasis added.

konzipieren oder abzuschirmen, dass unter Berücksichtigung der Betriebsfrequenz:

a. an Orten, die zwar innerhalb des Betriebsareals, aber ausserhalb von kontrollierten Zonen liegen und an denen sich nichtberuflich strahlenexponierte Personen aufhalten können, die Ortsdosis 0,02 mSv pro Woche nicht übersteigt. **Dieser Wert kann an Orten, wo sich Personen nicht dauernd aufhalten, bis zum Fünffachen überschritten werden**;
b. an Orten ausserhalb des Betriebsareals die Immissionsgrenzwerte nach Artikel 102 nicht überschritten werden.

[2] [...]

Art. 59 Shielding
[1] The room or area in which stationary radiation generators or radioactive sources are operated or stored shall be designed and shielded in such a way that, taking into account the frequency of use:

a. in places situated within the premises but outside controlled areas, where non-occupationally exposed persons may be present, the local dose does not exceed 0.02 mSv per week. **In places where people are not continuously present, this value may be exceeded by up to a factor of five**;
b. in places outside the premises, the off-site limits specified in Article102 are not exceeded.

[2] [...]

In this example, a parenthetical sentence (marked in bold face) has been inserted at the end of the first enumeration item. A full stop has been put where the main sentence is interrupted, whereas the inserted sentence is ended with a semicolon to indicate that after it, the main sentence is continued. The recognition of sentential insertions as the one shown in (2) is important for two reasons: (i) sentential parentheses are themselves the object of style rules (in general, they are to be avoided) and should thus be marked by a style checker, and (ii) a successful parsing of the texts depends on a proper recognition of the sentence boundaries. As off-the-shelf tools cannot cope with such domain-specific structures, we have had to devise highly specialised algorithms for sentence boundary detection in our texts.

4.3 Linguistic Analysis

Following text segmentation, we perform a linguistic analysis of the input text which consists of three components: part-of-speech tagging, lemmatisation and chunking/parsing. The information added by these pre-processing steps is later used in the detection of violations of style rules that pertain to the use of specific terms (e.g. "the modal *sollen* 'should' is to be avoided"), syntactic constructions (e.g. "complex participial constructions preceding a noun should be avoided") or combinations thereof (e.g. "obligations where the subject is an authority must be put as assertions and not contain a modal verb").

For the tasks of part-of-speech tagging and lemmatisation, we employ TreeTagger (Schmid, 1994). We have adapted TreeTagger to the peculiarities of Swiss legislative language. Domain-specific token types are pre-tagged in a special routine to avoid erroneous part-of-speech analyses. An example of a type of tokens that needs pre-tagging are domain-specific cardinal numbers: i.e. cardinal numbers augmented with letters (*Article 2a*) or with Latin ordinals (*Paragraph 4bis*) as well as ranges of such cardinal numbers (*Articles 3c–6*). Furthermore, TreeTagger's recognition of sentence boundaries is overwritten by the output of our text segmentation routine. We have also augmented TreeTagger's domain-general list of abbreviations with a list of domain-specific abbreviations and acronyms provided by the Swiss Federal Chancellery. The lemmatisation provided by TreeTagger usually does not recognise complex compound nouns (e.g. *Güterverkehrsverlagerung* 'freight traffic transfer'); such compound nouns are frequent in legislative texts (Nussbaumer, 2009). To solve the problem, we combine the output of TreeTagger's part-of-speech tagging with the lemma information delivered by the morphology analysis tool GERTWOL (Haapalainen and Majorin, 1995).

Some detection tasks (e.g. the detection of legal definitions discussed in section 4.4 below) additionally require chunking or even parsing. For chunking, we also employ TreeTagger; for parsing, we have begun to adapt ParZu to legislative language, a robust state-of-art dependency parser

(Sennrich et al., 2009). Like most off-the-shelf parsers, ParZu was trained on a corpus of newspaper articles. As a consequence, it struggles with analysing constructions that are rare in that domain but frequent in legislative texts, such as complex coordinations of prepositional phrases and PP-attachment chains (Venturi, 2008), parentheses (as illustrated in example 2 above) or subject clauses (as shown in example 3 below).

(3) *Art. 17 Rechtfertigender Notstand* [4]
Wer eine mit Strafe bedrohte Tat begeht, um ein eigenes oder das Rechtsgut einer anderen Person aus einer unmittelbaren, nicht anders abwendbaren Gefahr zu retten, handelt rechtmässig, wenn er dadurch höherwertige Interessen wahrt.

Art. 17 Legitimate act in a situation of necessity
Whoever carries out an act that carries a criminal penalty in order to save a legal interest of his own or of another from immediate and not otherwise avertable danger, acts lawfully if by doing so he safeguards interests of higher value.

As the adaptation of ParZu to legislative texts is still in its early stages, we cannot yet provide an assessment of how useful the output of the parser, once properly modified, will be to our task.

4.4 Context Recognition

The annotations that the pre-processing routines discussed so far add to the text serve as the basis for the automatic recognition of domain-specific contexts. Style rules for legislative drafting often only apply to special contexts within a law. An example is the rule pertaining to the use of the modal *sollen* ('should'). The drafting guidelines forbid the use of this modal *except* in statements of purpose. Statements of purpose thus constitute a special context inside which the detection of an instance of *sollen* is not to trigger an error message. Other examples of contexts in which special style rules apply are transitional provisions (*Übergangsbestimmungen*), repeals and amendments of current legislation (*Aufhebungen und Änderungen bisherigen Rechts*), definitions of the subject of a law (*Gegenstandsbestimmungen*), definitions of the scope of a law (*Geltungsbereichsbestimmungen*), definitions of terms (*Begriffsbestimmungen*), as well as preambles (*Präambeln*) and commencement clauses (*Ingresse*).

A number of these contexts can be identified automatically by assessing an article's position in the text and certain keywords contained in its header. A statements of purpose, for instance, is usually the first article of a law, and its header usually contains the words *Zweck* ('purpose') or *Ziel* ('aim'). Similar rules can be applied to recognise transitional provisions, repeals and amendments of current legislation, and definitions of the subject and the scope of a law.

Other contexts have to be detected at the sentential level. Definitions of terms, for instance, do not only occur as separate articles at the beginning of a law; they can also appear in the form of individual sentences throughout the text. As there is a whole range of style rules pertaining to legal definitions (e.g. "a term must only be defined if it occurs at least three times in the text"; "a term must only be defined once within the same text"; "a term must not be defined by itself"), the detection of this particular context (and its components: the term and the actual definition) is crucial to a style checker for legislative texts.[5]

To identify legal definitions in the text, we have begun to adopt strategies developed in the context of legal information retrieval: Walter and Pinkal (2009) and de Maat and Winkels (2010), for instance, show that definitions in German court decisions and in Dutch laws respectively can be detected by searching for combinations of key words and sentence patterns typically used in these domain-specific contexts. In Höfler et al. (2011) we have argued that this approach is also feasible with regard to Swiss legislative texts: our pilot study has shown that a substantial number of legal definitions can be detected even without resorting to syntactic analyses, merely by searching for typical string patterns such as *'X im Sinne dieser Verordnung ist/sind Y'* ('X in the sense of this ordinance is/are Y'). We are currently working towards refining and extending the detection of legal definitions by including additional syntactic information yielded by the processes of chunking and parsing into the search patterns.

[4] Strafgesetzbuch (Criminal Code), SR 311.0; emphasis added.

[5] Further rules for the use of legal definitions in Swiss law texts are provided by Bratschi (2009).

Once the legal definitions occurring in a draft have been marked, the aforementioned style rules can be checked automatically (e.g. by searching the text for terms that are defined in a definition but occur less than three times in the remainder of the text; by checking if there are any two legal definitions that define the same term; by assessing if there are definitions where the defined term also occurs in the actual definition).

After having outlined some of the main challenges that the peculiarities of legal language and legislative texts pose to the various pre-processing tasks, we now turn to the process of error modelling, i.e. the effort of transferring the guidelines for legislative drafting into concrete error detection mechanisms operating on the pre-processed texts.

5 Error Modelling

5.1 Sources

The first step towards error modelling consists in collecting the set of style rules that shall be applied to the input texts. The main source that we use for this purpose are the compilations of drafting guidelines published by the Swiss Federal Administration (Bundeskanzlei, 2003; Bundesamt für Justiz, 2007). However, especially when it comes to linguistic issues, these two documents do not claim to provide an exhaustive set of writing rules. Much more so than the writing rules that are put in place in the domain of technical documentation, the rules used in legislative drafting are based on historically grown conventions, and there may well be conventions beyond what is explicitly written down in the Federal Administration's official drafting guidelines.

Consequently, we have also been collecting rule material from three additional sources. A first complementary source are the various drafting guidelines issued by cantonal governments (Regierungsrat des Kantons Zürich, 2005; Regierungsrat des Kantons Bern, 2000) and, to a lesser extent, the drafting guidelines of the other German-speaking countries (Bundesministerium für Justiz, 2008; Bundeskanzleramt, 1990; Rechtsdienst der Regierung, 1990) and the European Union (Europäische Kommission, 2003). A second source are academic papers dealing with specific issues of legislative drafting, such as Eisenberg (2007), Bratschi (2009).

Finally, legislative editors themselves constitute an invaluable source of expert knowledge. In order to learn of their unwritten codes of practice, we have established a regular exchange with the Central Language Services of the Swiss Federal Chancellery. Including the editors in the process is likely to prove essential for the acceptability of the methods that we develop.

5.2 Concretisation and Formalisation

The next error modelling step consists in concretising and formalising the collected rules so that specific algorithms can be developed to search for violations of the rules in the pre-processed texts. Depending on the level of abstraction of a rule, this task is relatively straight-forward or it requires more extensive preliminary research:

Concrete Rules A number of rules for legislative drafting define concrete constraints and can thus be directly translated into detection rules. Examples of such concrete rules are rules that prohibit the use of specific abbreviations (e.g. *bzw.* 'respectively'; *z.B.* 'e.g.'; *d.h.* 'i.e.') and of certain terms and phrases (e.g. *grundsätzlich* 'in principle'; *in der Regel* 'as a general rule'). In such cases, error detection simply consists in searching for the respective items in the input text.

Some rules first need to be spelled out but can then also be formalised more or less directly: the rule stating that units of measurement must always be written out rather than abbreviated, for instance, requires that a list of such abbreviations of measuring units (e.g. *m* for meter, *kg* for kilogram, *%* for percent) is compiled whose entries can then be searched for in the text.

The formalisation of some other rules is somewhat more complicated but can still be derived more or less directly. The error detection strategies for these rules include accessing tags that were added during pre-processing or evaluating the environment of a potential error. For example, the rule stating that sentences introducing an enumeration must end in a colon can be checked by searching the text for `<enumeration>` tags that are *not* preceded by a colon; violations of the rule stating that an article must not contain more than three paragraphs can be detected by counting for each `<article_body>` environment, the number of `<paragraph>` elements it contains.

Abstract Rules However, guidelines for legislative drafting frequently contain rules that define relatively abstract constraints. In order to be able to detect violations of such constraints, a linguistic concretisation of the rules is required.

An example is the oft-cited rule that a sentence should only convey one statement or proposition (Bundesamt für Justiz, 2007, p. 358). The error modelling for this rule is not straightforward: it is neither clear what counts as a statement in the context of a legislative text, nor is it obvious what forms sentences violating this rule exhibit. Linguistic indicators for the presence of a multi-propositional sentence first need to be determined in in-depth analyses of legislative language. In Höfler (2011), we name a number of such indicators: among other things, sentence coordination, relative clauses introduced by the adverb *wobei* ('whereby'), and certain prepositions (e.g. *vorbehältlich* 'subject to' or *mit Ausnahme von* 'with the exception of') can be signs that a sentence contains more than one statement.

Even drafting rules that look fairly specific at first glance may turn out to be in need of further linguistic concretisation. An example is the rule that states that in an enumeration, words that are shared between all enumeration elements should be bracketed out into the introductory sentence of the enumeration. If, for instance, each element of an enumeration starts with the preposition *für* ('for'), then that preposition belongs in the introductory sentence. The rule seems straight enough, but in reality, the situation is somewhat more complicated. Example (4) shows a case where a word that occurs at the beginning of all elements of an enumeration (the definite article *die* 'the') cannot be bracketed out into the introductory sentence:

(4) *Art. 140 Obligatorisches Referendum*[6]
[...]
[2] Dem Volk werden zur Abstimmung unterbreitet:

a. **die** Volksinitiativen auf Totalrevision der Bundesverfassung;
b. **die** Volksinitiativen auf Teilrevision der Bundesverfassung in der Form der allgemeinen Anregung, die von der Bundesversammlung abgelehnt worden sind;
c. **die** Frage, ob eine Totalrevision der Bundesverfassung durchzuführen ist, bei Uneinigkeit der beiden Räte.

Art. 140 Mandatory referendum
[...]
[2] The following shall be submitted to a vote of the People:

a. **the** popular initiatives for a complete revision of the Federal Constitution;
b. **the** popular initiatives for a partial revision of the Federal Constitution in the form of a general proposal that have been rejected by the Federal Assembly;
c. **the** question of whether a complete revision of the Federal Constitution should be carried out, in the event that there is disagreement between the two Councils.

Even if one ignores the fact that the definite article in letters *a* and *b* is in fact not the same as the one in letter *c* (the former being plural, the latter singular), it is quite apparent that articles cannot be extracted from the elements of an enumeration without the nouns they specify. Even the seemingly simple rule in question is thus in need of a more linguistically informed concretisation before it can be effectively checked by machine.

The examples illustrate that style guidelines for legislative writing are often kept at a level of abstraction that necessitates concretisations if one is to detect violations of the respective rules automatically. Besides the development of domain-specific pre-processing algorithms, the extensive and highly specialised linguistic research required for such concretisations constitutes the main task being tackled in this project.

Conflicting Rules A further challenge to error modelling arises from the fact that a large proportion of drafting guidelines for legislative texts do not constitute absolute constraints but rather have the status of general writing principles and rules of thumb. This fact has to be reflected in the feedback messages that the system gives to its users: what the tool detects are often not "errors" in the proper sense of the word but merely passages that the author or editor may want to reconsider.

The fact that many style rules only define soft constraints also means that there may be conflicting rules. Consider, for instance, sentence (5):

[6] Bundesverfassung (Federal Constitution), SR 101; emphasis added.

(5) *Art. 36 Ersatzfreiheitsstrafe*[7]
[...]
[5] Soweit der Verurteilte die Geldstrafe trotz verlängerter Zahlungsfrist oder herabgesetztem Tagessatz nicht bezahlt oder die gemeinnützige Arbeit trotz Mahnung nicht leistet, wird die Ersatzfreiheitsstrafe vollzogen.

Art. 36 Alternative custodial sentence
[...]
[5] As far as the offender fails to pay the monetary penalty despite being granted an extended deadline for payment or a reduced daily penalty unit or fails to perform the community service despite being warned of the consequences, the alternative custodial sentence is executed.

On the one hand, this sentence must be considered a violation of the style rule that states that the main verb of a sentence (here *execute*) should be introduced as early as possible (Regierungsrat des Kantons Zürich, 2005, p. 73). On the other hand, if the sentence was re-arranged in compliance with this rule – by switching the order of the main clause and the subsidiary clause – it would violate the rule stating that information is to be presented in temporal and causal order (Bundesamt für Justiz, 2007, p. 354). This latter rule entails that the condition precedes its consequence.

To be able to deal with such conflicting constraints, error detection strategies have to be assigned weights. However, one and the same rule may have different weights under different circumstances. In conditional sentences like the one shown above, the causality principle obviously weighs more than the rule that the main verb must be introduced early in the sentence. Such context-dependent rankings for individual style rules have to be inferred and corroborated by tailor-made corpus-linguistic studies.

5.3 Testing and Evaluation

The number of drafts available to us is very limited – too limited to be used to test and refine the error models we develop. However, due to the complexity of the drafting process (multiple authors and editors, political intervention), laws that have already come into force still exhibit violations of specific style rules. We therefore resort to such already published laws to test and refine the error models we develop. To this aim, we have built a large corpus of legislative texts automatically annotated by the pre-processing routines we have described earlier in the paper (Höfler and Piotrowski, 2011). The corpus contains the entire current federal legislation of Switzerland, i.e. the federal constitution, all cantonal constitutions, all federal acts and ordinances, federal decrees and treaties between the Confederation and individual cantons and municipalities. It allows us to try out and evaluate novel error detection strategies by assessing the number and types of true and false positives returned.

[7] Strafgesetzbuch (Criminal Code), SR 311.0

6 Conclusion

In this paper, we have discussed the development of methods for the automated detection of violations of domain-specific style guidelines for legislative texts, and their implementation in a prototypical tool. We have illustrated how the approach of error modelling employed in automated style checkers for technical writing can be enhanced to meet the requirements of legislative editing. Two main sets of challenges are tackled in this process. First, domain-specific NLP methods for legislative drafts have to be provided. Without extensive adaptations, off-the-shelf NLP tools that have been trained on corpora of newspaper articles are not adequately equipped to deal with the peculiarities of legal language and legislative texts. Second, the error modelling for a large number of drafting guidelines requires a concretisation step before automated error detection strategies can be put in place. The substantial linguistic research that such concretisations require constitutes a core task to be carried out in the development of a style checker for legislative texts.

Acknowledgments

The project is funded under SNSF grant 134701. The authors wish to thank the Central Language Services of the Swiss Federal Chancellery for their continued advice and support.

References

Rebekka Bratschi. 2009. "Frau im Sinne dieser Badeordnung ist auch der Bademeister." Legaldefinitionen aus redaktioneller Sicht. *LeGes*, 20(2):191–213.

Bundesamt für Justiz, editor. 2007. *Gesetzgebungsleitfaden: Leitfaden für die Ausarbeitung von Erlassen des Bundes*. Bern, 3. edition.

Bundeskanzlei, editor. 2003. *Gesetzestechnische Richtlinien*. Bern.

Bundeskanzleramt, editor. 1990. *Handbuch der Rechtsetzungstechnik, Teil 1: Legistische Leitlinien*. Wien.

Bundesministerium für Justiz, editor. 2008. *Handbuch der Rechtsförmlichkeit, Empfehlungen zur Gestaltung von Gesetzen und Rechtsverordnungen*. Bundesanzeiger Verlag, Köln.

Peter Butt and Richard Castle. 2006. *Modern Legal Drafting*. Cambridge University Press, Cambridge, UK, 2nd edition.

Emile de Maat and Radboud Winkels. 2010. Automated classification of norms in sources of law. In *Semantic Processing of Legal Texts*. Springer, Berlin.

Karin M. Eichhoff-Cyrus and Gerd Antos, editors. 2008. *Verständlichkeit als Bürgerrecht? Die Rechts- und Verwaltungssprache in der öffentlichen Diskussion*. Duden, Mannheim, Germany.

Peter Eisenberg. 2007. Die Grammatik der Gesetzessprache: Was ist eine Verbesserung? In Andreas Lötscher and Markus Nussbaumer, editors, *Denken wie ein Philosoph und schreiben wie ein Bauer*, pages 105–122. Schulthess, Zürich.

Europäische Kommission, editor. 2003. *Gemeinsamer Leitfaden des Europäischen Parlaments, des Rates und der Kommission für Personen, die in den Gemeinschaftsorganen an der Abfassung von Rechtstexten mitwirken*. Amt für Veröffentlichungen der Europäischen Gemeinschaften, Luxemburg.

Stephanie Geldbach. 2009. Neue Werkzeuge zur Autorenunterstützung. *MDÜ*, 4:10–19.

Mariikka Haapalainen and Ari Majorin. 1995. GERTWOL und morphologische Desambiguierung für das Deutsche. In *Proceedings of the 10th Nordic Conference of Computational Linguistics*. University of Helsinki, Department of General Linguistics.

Stefan Höfler and Michael Piotrowski. 2011. Building corpora for the philological study of Swiss legal texts. *Journal for Language Technology and Computational Linguistics (JLCL)*, 26(2):77–90.

Stefan Höfler, Alexandra Bünzli, and Kyoko Sugisaki. 2011. Detecting legal definitions for automated style checking in draft laws. Technical Report CL-2011.01, University of Zurich, Institute of Computational Linguistics, Zürich.

Stefan Höfler. 2011. "Ein Satz – eine Aussage." Multipropositionale Rechtssätze an der Sprache erkennen. *LeGes*, 22(2):259–279.

Anne Lehrndorfer. 1996. *Kontrolliertes Deutsch: Linguistische und sprachpsychologische Leitlinien für eine (maschinell) kontrollierte Sprache in der Technischen Dokumentation*. Günter Narr, Tübingen.

Kent D. Lerch, editor. 2004. *Recht verstehen. Verständlichkeit, Missverständlichkeit und Unverständlichkeit von Recht*. de Gruyter, Berlin.

Maria Mindlin. 2005. Is plain language better? A comparative readability study of plain language court forms. *Scribes Journal of Legal Writing*, 10.

Uwe Muegge. 2007. Controlled language: The next big thing in translation? *ClientSide News Magazine*, 7(7):21–24.

Markus Nussbaumer. 2009. Rhetorisch-stilistische Eigenschaften der Sprache des Rechtswesens. In Ulla Fix, Andreas Gardt, and Joachim Knape, editors, *Rhetorik und Stilistik/Rhetoric and Stylistics*, Handbooks of Linguistics and Communication Science, pages 2132–2150. de Gruyter, New York/Berlin.

Rechtsdienst der Regierung, editor. 1990. *Richtlinien der Regierung des Fürstentums Liechtenstein über die Grundsätze der Rechtsetzung (Legistische Richtlinien)*. Vaduz.

Regierungsrat des Kantons Bern, editor. 2000. *Rechtsetzungsrichtlinien des Kantons Bern*. Bern.

Regierungsrat des Kantons Zürich, editor. 2005. *Richtlinien der Rechtsetzung*. Zürich.

Ursula Reuther. 2003. Two in one – can it work? Readability and translatability by means of controlled language. In *Proceedings of EAMT-CLAW 2003*.

Helmut Schmid. 1994. Probabilistic part-of-speech tagging using decision trees. In *Proceedings of the International Conference on New Methods in Language Processing*, pages 44–49.

Rico Sennrich, Gerold Schneider, Martin Volk, and Martin Warin. 2009. A new hybrid dependency parser for German. In *Proceedings of the GSCL Conference 2009*, pages 115–124, Tübingen.

Giulia Venturi. 2008. Parsing legal texts: A contrastive study with a view to knowledge managment applications. In *Proceedings of the LREC 2008 Workshop on Semantic Processing of Legal Texts*, pages 1–10, Marakesh.

Stephan Walter and Manfred Pinkal. 2009. Definitions in court decisions: Automatic extraction and ontology acquisition. In Joost Breuker, Pompeu Casanovas, Michel Klein, and Enrico Francesconi, editors, *Law, Ontologies and the Semantic Web*. IOS Press, Amsterdam.

Richard C. Wydick. 2005. *Plain English for Lawyers*. Carolina Academic Press, 5th edition.

Aggregated Assessment and "Objectivity 2.0"

Joseph M. Moxley
University of South Florida
4202 East Fowler Avenue
Tampa, FL, USA 33620
moxley@usf.edu

Abstract

This essay provides a summary of research related to *My Reviewers*, a web-based application that can be used for teaching and assessment purposes. The essay concludes with speculation about ongoing development efforts, including a social helpfulness algorithm, a badging system, and Natural Language Processing (NLP) features.

1 Introduction

The essay summarizes research that has identified ways *My Reviewers* can be used to:

- integrate formative with summative evaluations, thereby enabling universities and teachers to alter curriculum approaches in real time in response to ongoing assessment information,
- assess students' critical thinking, research, and writing skills—aggregating not a small percentage but all of the marked up documents (in our case about 16,000 evaluations by teachers of students' intermediate and final drafts of essays/semester),
- enable reviewers (teachers and students) to provide more objective feedback, facilitating "Objectivity 2.0," a form of evaluative consensus mediated after extensive crowdsourcing of standards,
- provide conclusive evidence that can be used to compare the efficacy of particular curricular approaches,
- enable students and writing programs to track progress related to specific learning outcomes (from project to project, course to course, year to year),
- inform faculty development and teacher response, and
- create an e-portfolio of students' work that reflects their ongoing progress.

2 What is *My Reviewers*?

My Reviewers is a web-based application that enables students, teachers, and universities to

- aggregate assessment information about students' critical thinking and writing skills,
- mark up PDF documents (with sticky notes, text box notes, drawing tools, etc.),
- grade documents according to a rubric,
- assign and conduct or grade peer reviews. (My Reviewers enables teachers to see at a glance each student's in-text annotations, end-note comments, and rubric scores),
- use a library of comments and resources tailored to address common writing problems, and
- crowdsource comments and resources.

The permissions-based workflow features of *My Reviewers* enable teachers and students to use a rubric and commenting tools to review and grade student writing while protecting student confidentiality behind a Net ID.

My Reviewers is founded on the assumptions that language and learning are social practices, and that students can provide valuable feedback to one another based on their backgrounds as readers and critical thinkers.

By enabling students to track their progress (or lack of progress) according to various evaluative criteria (such as focus, evidence, organization, style, and format), *My Reviewers* clarifies academic expectations and facilitates reflection and awareness of teachers' evaluations and concerns, thereby helping students grow as writers, editors, and collaborators. Furthermore, the pedagogical materials embedded into the tool—videos, explanatory materials, exercises, library of comments with supporting hyperlinks—clarify

Proceedings of the EACL 2012 Workshop on Computational Linguistics and Writing, pages 19–26,
Avignon, France, April 23, 2012. ©2012 Association for Computational Linguistics

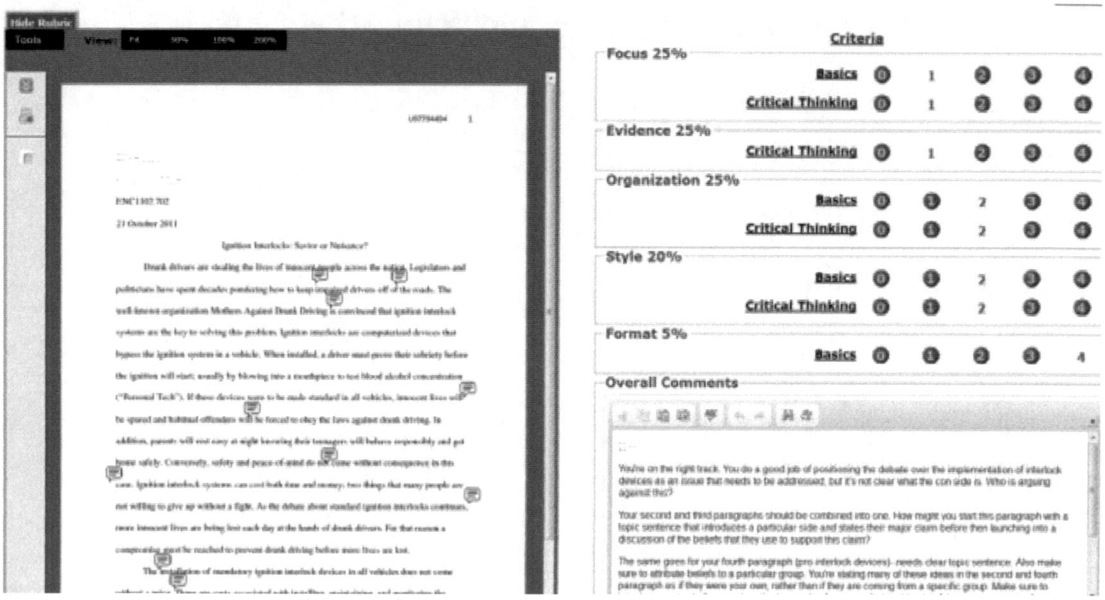

Figure 1: Sample Document Markup and Rubric

grading criteria for both students and teachers. In summary, by aggregating assessment results in innovative new ways, *My Reviewers* reshapes how teachers respond to writing, how students conduct peer reviews, how students track their development as writers and reader feedback, and how universities can conduct assessments of students' development as critical thinkers and writers.

3 Context and Methods

The FYC (First-Year Composition) Program at the University of South Florida is one of the largest writing programs in the U.S, serving approximately 7,500 students in two composition courses each year, ENC 1101 and ENC 1102. Thanks to funding from USF Tech Fee Funds and CTE21, we have piloted use of *My Reviewers* for the past three years, using *My Reviewers* to assess over 30,000 student documents. Last semester (Fall 2011), approximately 70 first-year composition instructors assessed 16,000 essays (including early, intermediate, and final drafts)—not counting student peer reviews. This semester (Spring 2012), we are on course for reviewing another 16,000 essays. The National Council of Teachers of English awarded the FYC Program the *2011-12 CCCC (Conference on College Composition and Communication) Writing Program Certificate of Excellence Award* based in part on its development of *My Reviewers*.

Over the past eight years, our teachers and writing program administrators have crowd-sourced a community rubric by employing various peer-production technologies and face-to-face meetings (see Table 1). The early stages of our development process are reported in Vieregge, Stedman, Mitchell, & Moxley's (2012) *Agency in the Age of Peer Production*, an ethnographic monograph published by NCTE's series on Studies in Writing and Rhetoric.

Since moving from a requirement for our instructors to use a printed version of the community rubric to using *My Reviewers,* which enables teachers to view the rubric while grading and associates rubric scores with marked-up texts, we have observed some benefits: While we may have 500 sections of the 1101 and 1102 courses, we want all of these sections to focus on shared outcomes. We have found our use of *My Reviewers* helps ensure students have a more comparable experience than when paper rubrics were used. Back in the days of the printed version of the rubric, at the end of the semester when we surveyed students about usage, about half of our students reported they were unfamiliar with the rubric. One of the advantages of an online tool like *My Reviewers* for universities is that it enables writing program administrators to better ensure instructors and students are keeping up with our shared curriculum. Also, by using a single analytic rubric tool across sections, we can assess progress by student, teacher, section, and rubric criteria.

Criteria	Level	Emerging 0	1	Developing 2	3	Mastering 4
Focus	*Basics*	Does not meet assignment requirements		Partially meets assignment requirements		Meets assignment requirements
	Critical Thinking	Absent or weak thesis; ideas are underdeveloped, vague or unrelated to thesis; poor analysis of ideas relevant to thesis		Predictable or unoriginal thesis; ideas are partially developed and related to thesis; inconsistent analysis of subject relevant to thesis		Insightful/intriguing thesis; ideas are convincing and compelling; cogent analysis of subject relevant to thesis
Evidence	*Critical Thinking*	Sources and supporting details lack credibility; poor synthesis of primary and secondary sources/evidence relevant to thesis; poor synthesis of visuals/personal experience/anecdotes relevant to thesis; rarely distinguishes between writer's ideas and source's ideas		Fair selection of credible sources and supporting details; unclear relationship between thesis and primary and secondary sources/evidence; ineffective synthesis of sources/evidence relevant to thesis; occasionally effective synthesis of visuals/personal experience/anecdotes relevant to thesis; inconsistently distinguishes between writer's ideas and source's ideas		Credible and useful sources and supporting details; cogent synthesis of primary and secondary sources/evidence relevant to thesis; clever synthesis of visuals/personal experience/anecdotes relevant to thesis; distinguishes between writer's ideas and source's ideas.
Organization	*Basics*	Confusing opening; absent, inconsistent, or non-relevant topic sentences; few transitions and absent or unsatisfying conclusion		Uninteresting or somewhat trite introduction, inconsistent use of topics sentences, segues, transitions, and mediocre conclusion		Engaging introduction, relevant topic sentences, good segues, appropriate transitions, and compelling conclusion
	Critical Thinking	Illogical progression of supporting points; lacks cohesiveness		Supporting points follow a somewhat logical progression; occasional wandering of ideas; some interruption of cohesiveness		Logical progression of supporting points; very cohesive
Style	*Basics*	Frequent grammar/punctuation errors; inconsistent point of view		Some grammar/punctuation errors occur in some places; somewhat consistent point of view		Correct grammar and punctuation; consistent point of view
	Critical Thinking	Significant problems with syntax, diction, word choice, and vocabulary		Occasional problems with syntax, diction, word choice, and vocabulary		Rhetorically-sound syntax, diction, word choice, and vocabulary; effective use of figurative language
Format	*Basics*	Little compliance with accepted documentation style (i.e., MLA, APA) for paper formatting, in-text citations, annotated bibliographies, and works cited; minimal attention to document design		Inconsistent compliance with accepted documentation style (i.e., MLA, APA) for paper formatting, in-text citations, annotated bibliographies, and works cited; some attention to document design		Consistent compliance with accepted documentation style (i.e., MLA, APA) for paper formatting, in-text citations, annotated bibliographies, and works cited; strong attention to document design

Table 1: Community Assessment Rubric

As rhetoricians, we understand the value of using rubrics that address the demands of specific rhetorical contexts. When addressing different genres, audiences, disciplines and when using multiple media to remediate texts (Twitter, podcasts, movies, print documents), students clearly benefit from receiving feedback related to conventions in those genres, disciplines, and media. Given this, we clearly understand why Peter Elbow, Chris Anson, William Condon, among other assessment leaders, fault universities for employing a generic rubric like our community rubric to assess texts across projects, genres, courses, media and so on. Like Elbow (2006), Anson (2011), and Condon (2011), we see enormous value in clarifying specific grading criteria for specific projects, and we understand grading criteria change along with changes in different rhetorical situations. Plus, as compositionists, we understand that writers need different kinds of feedback when they are in different stages of the composing process. Using a rubric like our community rubric early in the writing process can clearly be overkill. There is no point in discussing style, for example, when the writer needs to be told that his or her purpose is unclear or not satisfactory given the assignment specifications. Nonetheless, we have found—as we discuss below—some benefits for using our community rubric to assess multiple projects, even ones that address different audiences, genres, and media.

4 Independent Validation of the Community Rubric by the USF Office of Institutional Effectiveness

While we are currently seeking funding to add administration features that would enable users to write their own rubrics or import rubrics, *My Reviewers* employs a single community rubric (see Table 1) that has been validated by an independent assessment conducted by the Office of Institutional Effectiveness at the University of South Florida in the spring of 2010.

To conduct the assessment, 10 independent scorers reviewed the third/final drafts of 249 students' ENC 1101 Project 2 essays and these same students' ENC 1102 Project 2 essays. The Office of Institutional Effectiveness settled on this odd number—249—because it represented 5% of our total *unique* student head count (4,980 students) for the 2009/2010 academic year. The scorers used the same scoring rubric to evaluate all 498 essays according to eight criteria delineated in our community rubric. Scorers did not provide comments nor did they have access to the markup and grading provided by the students' classroom instructors.

Before the raters scored the randomly chosen student essays, an assessment expert from the Office of Institutional Effectiveness led a brief discussion of the rubric and asked the scorers to read sample essays. He then computed an inter-rater agreement of .93. Confident our scorers understood our rubric and encouraged by our inter-rater reliability, raters subsequently scored the 498 essays over a three-day period.

Naturally, we were pleased to see that our assessment results suggested students were making some progress on all measures of writing and critical thinking, that their 1102 Project 2 scores were higher than their Project 2 scores in 1101, although we were underwhelmed by the degree of improvement. We also were not really surprised that we were able to reach a high level of inter-rater reliability among raters.

However, this study did reveal a counterintuitive and remarkable result: by comparing the rankings of the independent scorers with the rankings of these students' classroom teachers, *we found no statistical difference on seven of the eight rubric criteria*. In other words, when it came to scoring eight criteria, the only difference between the independent scorers and the classroom teachers was "Style (Basics)," a criterion that represents a 5% grade weight when the rubric was used to grade student papers. This discrepancy may suggest that the independent scorers were being more lenient regarding the students' grammatical and stylistic infelicities than the students' classroom teachers.

Overall, the high level of agreement among the classroom teachers and the independent scorers suggests *My Reviewers* (perhaps by clarifying the grading criteria for teachers and students) enables diverse reviewers to mediate a shared evaluation of texts, to reach an unprecedented level of inter-rater reliability among large groups of readers—what we might call "Objectivity 2.0."

In a recent exchange on the Writing Program Administrator Listserv, Chris Anson, this year's Chair of the Conference on College Composition and past president of the Writing Program Administrators writes: "[the] Problem with [generic] rubrics is their usual high level of generalization (which makes them worthless)." In a subsequent co-authored essay, *"Big Rubrics and Weird Genres: The Futility of Using Generic Assessment Tools Across Diverse Instructional Contexts,"* Anson *et. al.* (in press) write: "Put simply, generic, all-purpose criteria for evaluating writing and oral communication fail to reflect the linguistic, rhetorical, relational, and contextual characteristics of specific kinds of writing or speaking that we find in higher education."

While we share Anson's preferences for rubrics that are designed to address the particular conventions of specific genres, audiences and media, and while we hope to secure the funding we need to add greater flexibility to *My Reviewers*—so we can better account for different rhetorical situations and media—, our research demonstrates the value and credibility of using a community rubric to assess multiple genres, even ones that are quite distinct, such as the personal narrative essays versus third-person based research reports. Perhaps our results suggest that the eight criteria defined by our rubric are generalizable enough across disciplines, genres, and media that university faculty can recognize them and employ them in meaningful ways to reach Objectivity 2.0.

To be completely frank, we are somewhat astounded by the inter-rater reliability we have been able to achieve among such diverse readers, and we wonder whether a rubric such as our community rubric can be used meaningfully to overcome the "courseocentrism" that Gerald Graff (2010) has described as undermining education in the U.S. Perhaps a tool such as *My Reviewers* can be used to leverage communication across departments, perhaps general-education wide, to address the common characteristics of academic prose that faculty across disciplines value.

5 Assess Undergraduate Learning

Richard Arum and Josipa Roksa have received worldwide attention for their evidence and argument in *Academically Adrift* (2011) that undergraduates fail to learn much despite their coursework. In contrast, by comparing students' scores from project to project, we have been able to demonstrate students' development as writers, researchers, and critical thinkers. Note, for example, our evidence, shown in Figure 2, of student development over one academic semester—based not on a small sample size but on *all* students in ENC 1102 that semester.

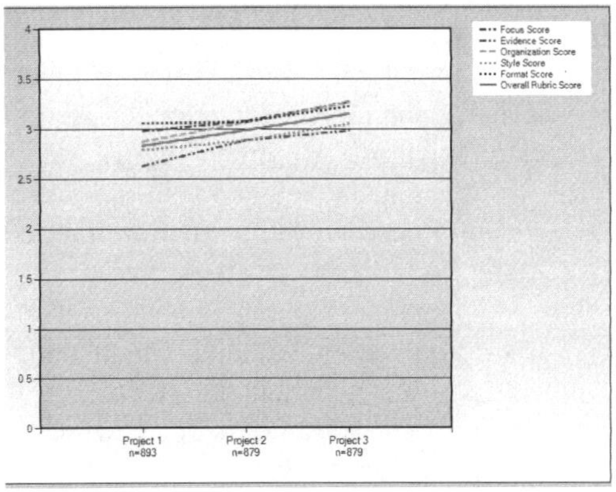

Figure 2: 1102 Final Project Scores

6 Make Evidence-Based Curriculum Changes

As any seasoned teacher or administrator knows, not all curricular materials are equivalent. On occasion, students perform poorly not because of a lack of innate inability but because of poor curricular planning on the part of the teachers (e.g., inadequate scaffolding of projects). Figure 3 illustrates ways *My Reviewers* can be used to improve the curriculum in light of evidence—illustrating ways assessment results can be used to inform curriculum changes. In this example, program administrators made changes to the historiography project (Project 2) from the Spring 2010 semester, and, subsequently, in the Fall 2011 semester students scored significantly better on most measures (Langbehn, McIntyre, Moxley, 2012).

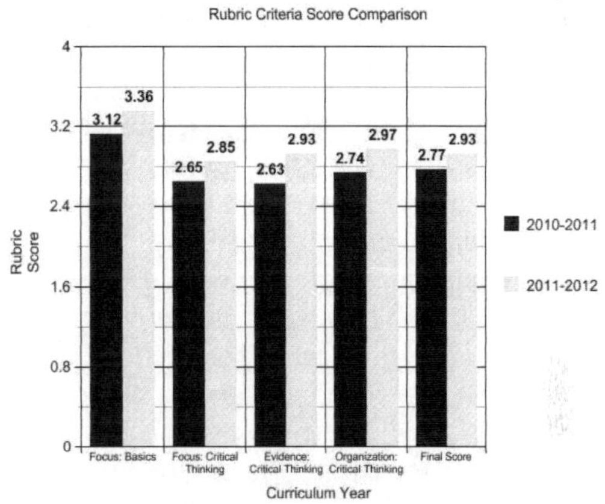

Figure 3: Comparison of Project 2 for the Spring 2010 vs. Fall 2011 Semesters

7 Compare Alternative Curricular Approaches

Use of a community rubric across genres, courses and disciplines can also be used to chart student progress, or lack of progress, or to indicate distinctions between the levels of difficulty imposed by unique projects/genres. On occasion, the lack of student success can be linked to issues pertaining to curriculum design as opposed to a particular student deficit. Figure 4 shows the comparison of student scores in two alternative courses, taken in succession by students at our university—results that suggest we need to once again rethink our curriculum for 1101 despite our intuition that the course was well designed and well received:

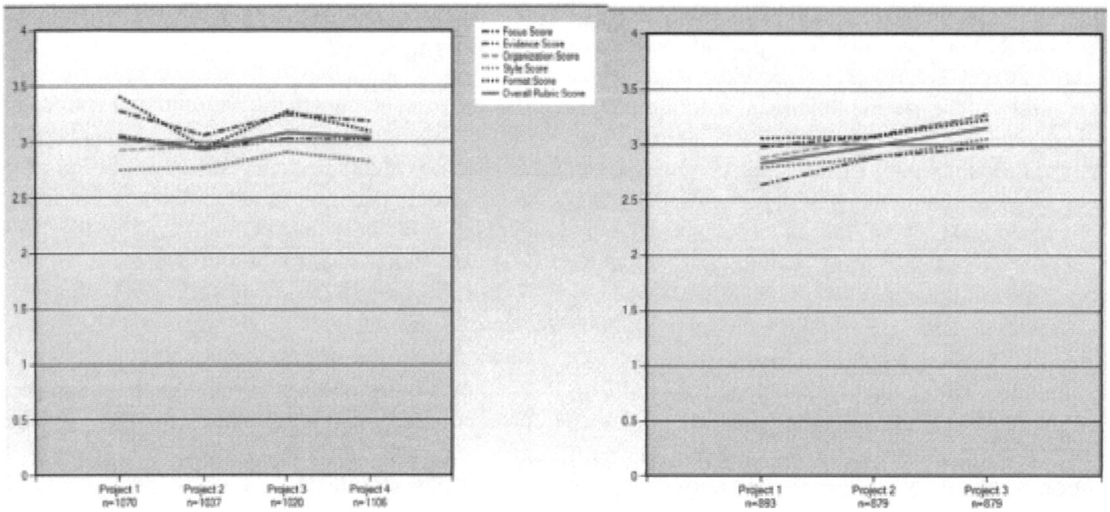

Figure 4: 1101 (left) vs. 1102 Final Project Results

8 Develop and Compare New Models for Teaching and Learning

Writing programs can use tools such as *My Reviewers* to compare alternative curriculums. We are currently providing three alternative approaches to teaching writing in university settings—the traditional approach, where students meet three hours each week in class; an online model; and a collaborative model, which requires students to use *My Reviewers* to conduct two cycles of peer review and two cycles of teacher feedback—as illustrated partially in Figure 5.

9 NLP Features Under Development

We are currently implementing a library of comments, which we developed by analyzing approximately 30,000 annotations and 20,000 endnotes; we are in the process of developing resources to help students better understand teacher and peer comments.

We are seeking additional funding to develop an algorithm and badging system to inspire more effective peer-review. By enabling students to earn badges according to the quality of their feedback, as measured by their peers and students, we are hoping to provide a further incentive for quality feedback. We would like to tie the badges to the number of substantive and editorial critiques that the document authors account for when revising, by endorsements by teachers for peer feedback, and by overall rankings of peer reviews.

Eventually we hope to add NLP (Natural Language Processing) tools that identify repeated patterns of error—as identified by past and present teachers who have used the tool. For example, students could be informed when they have received similar feedback in the past, and they could be offered hyperlinks back to past, similar comments. We can imagine features that highlight for teachers common comments on specific sets of papers or projects. Perhaps OER (Open Education Resources) such as Writing Commons, http://writingcommons.org, could be suggested as teachers and peers make comments.

10 Conclusions

In his seminal work, *The Wealth of Networks,* Yochai Benkler wisely remarks,

> Different technologies make different kinds of human action and interaction easier or harder to perform. All other things being equal, things that are easier to do are more likely to be done, and things that are harder to do are less likely to be done. (17)

My Reviewers, and other tools like it that are in development, shatter pedagogical practices by making it easier to provide comments, easier to organize and grade peer reviews, and easier to conduct assessments based on whole populations rather than randomly selected groups. The Learning Analytics embedded in tools like *My Reviewers* can empower students, teachers, and administrators in meaningful ways.

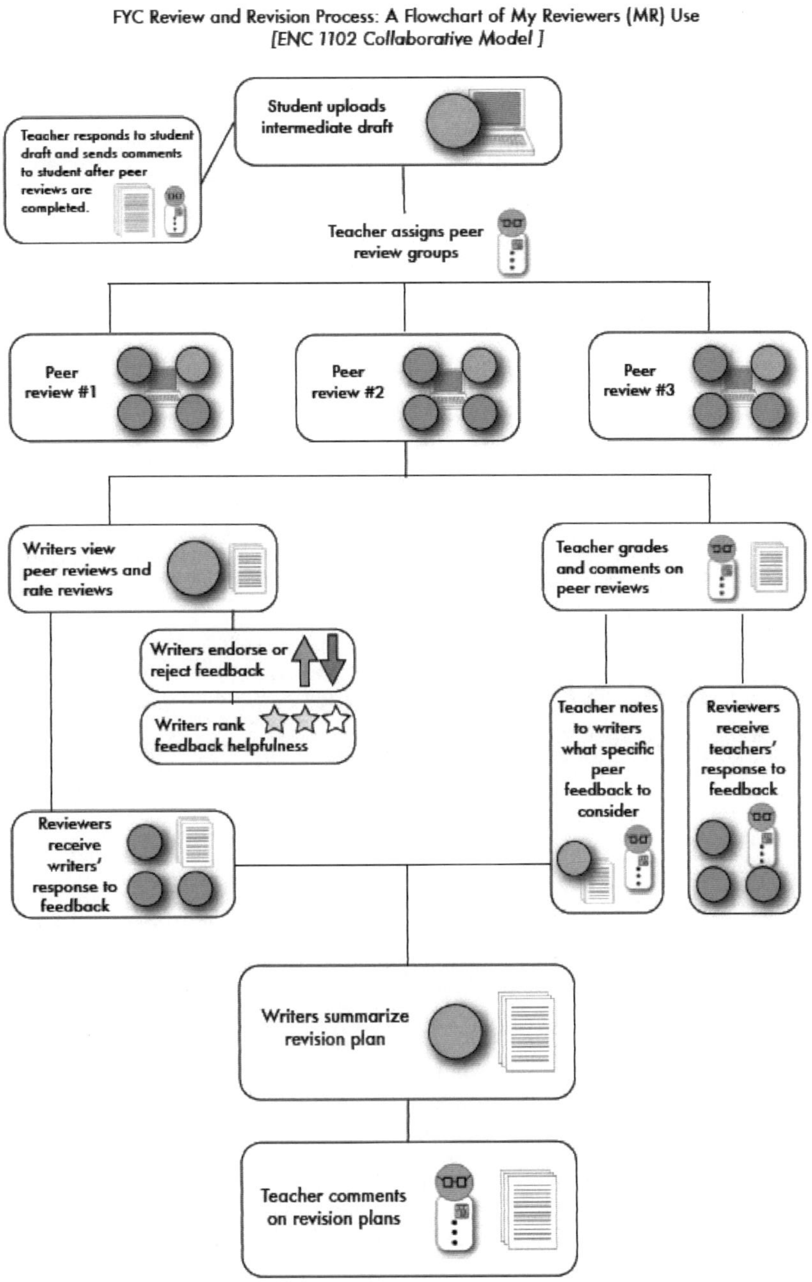

Figure 5: Cycle 1 for Peer Review Process

Acknowledgments

Project Development has been a deeply collaborative effort. Terry Beavers, Mike Shuman, and I—the chief architects of *My Reviewers*—have benefitted from the contributions of many colleagues. We thank Michelle Flanagan, for her ongoing development work; Dianne Donnelly; Hunt Hawkins; Janet Moore; Steve RiCharde; Dianne Williams; Nancy Serrano, Megan McIntyre; Nancy Lewis; Brianna Jerman; Erin Trauth.

Finally, we thank the University of South Florida Technology Fee Grant Program and the Center for 21st Century Teaching Excellence for funding our project.

References

Chris M. Anson. 2011. Re: Rubrics and writing assessment. In WPA-L Archives. Council of Writing Program Administrators. Message posted to http://wpacouncil.org/wpa-l

Chris M. Anson, Deanna P. Dannels, Pamela Flash, & A.L.H. Gaffney. In press. Big Rubrics and Weird Genres: The Futility of Using Generic Assessment Tools Across Diverse Instructional Contexts. Journal of Writing Assessment.

Richard Arum & Josipa Roksa. 2011. Academically Adrift. University of Chicago Press, Chicago.

Yochai Benkler. 2006. The Wealth of Networks. Yale University Press, New Haven and London.

William F. Condon. 2011. Re: Rubrics and writing assessment. In WPA-L Archives. Council of Writing Program Administrators. Message posted to http://wpacouncil.org/wpa-l

Peter Elbow. 2006. Do We Need a Single Standard of Value for Institutional Assessment? An Essay Response to Asao Inoue's 'Community-Based Assessment Pedagogy'. Assessing Writing, 11:81–99.

Gerald Graff. 2010. Why Assessment? Pedagogy, 12(1):153-165.

Karen Langbehn, Megan McIntyre & Joseph Moxley. Under review. Using Real-Time Formative Assessments to Close the Assessment Loop. In Heidi McKee & Danielle Nicole DeVoss (Eds.), Digital Writing Assessment.

Quentin Vieregge, Kyle Stedman, Taylor Mitchell, and Joseph Moxley.. In press. Agency in the Age of Peer Production. Studies in Writing and Rhetoric Series. National Council of Teachers of English, Urbana, IL.

Google Books N-gram Corpus used as a Grammar Checker

Rogelio Nazar **Irene Renau**
University Institute of Applied Linguistics
Universitat Pompeu Fabra
Roc Boronat 138
08018 Barcelona, Spain
{rogelio.nazar,irene.renau}@upf.edu

Abstract

In this research we explore the possibility of using a large n-gram corpus (Google Books) to derive lexical transition probabilities from the frequency of word n-grams and then use them to check and suggest corrections in a target text without the need for grammar rules. We conduct several experiments in Spanish, although our conclusions also reach other languages since the procedure is corpus-driven. The paper reports on experiments involving different types of grammar errors, which are conducted to test different grammar-checking procedures, namely, spotting possible errors, deciding between different lexical possibilities and filling-in the blanks in a text.

1 Introduction

This paper discusses a series of early experiments on a methodology for the detection and correction of grammatical errors based on co-occurrence statistics using an extensive corpus of n-grams (Google Books, compiled by Michel et al., 2011). We start from two complementary assumptions: on the one hand, books are published accurately, that is to say, they usually go through different phases of revision and correction with high standards and thus a large proportion of these texts can be used as a reference corpus for inferring the grammar rules of a language. On the other hand, we hypothesise that with a sufficiently large corpus a high percentage of the information about these rules can be extracted with word n-grams. Thus, although there are still many grammatical errors that cannot be detected with this method, there is also another important group which can be identified and corrected successfully, as we will see in Section 4.

Grammatical errors are the most difficult and complex type of language errors, because grammar is made up of a very extensive number of rules and exceptions. Furthermore, when grammar is observed in actual texts, the panorama becomes far more complicated, as the number of exceptions grows and the variety and complexity of syntactical structures increase to an extent that is not predicted by theoretical studies of grammar. Grammar errors are extremely important, and the majority of them cannot be considered to be performance-based because it is the meaning of the text and therefore, the success or failure of communication, that is compromised.

To our knowledge, no grammar book or dictionary has yet provided a solution to all the problems a person may have when he or she writes and tries to follow the grammar rules of language. Doubts that arise during the writing process are not always clearly associated to a lexical unit, or the writer is not able to detect such an association, and this makes it difficult to find the solution using a reference book.

In recent years, some advances have been made in the automatic detection of grammar mistakes (see Section 2). Effective rule-based methods have been reported, but at the cost of a very time-consuming task and with an inherent lack of flexibility. In contrast, statistical methods are easier and faster to implement, as well as being more flexible and adaptable. The experiment we will describe in the following sections is the first part of a more extensive study. Most probably, the logical step to follow in order to continue such a study will be a hybrid approach, based on both

Proceedings of the EACL 2012 Workshop on Computational Linguistics and Writing, pages 27–34,
Avignon, France, April 23, 2012. ©2012 Association for Computational Linguistics

statistics and rules. Hence, this paper aims to contribute to the statistical approach applied to grammar checking.

The Google Books N-gram Corpus is a database of n-grams of sequences of up to 5 words and records the frequency distribution of each unit in each year from 1500 onwards. The bulk of the corpus, however, starts from 1970, and that is the year we took as a starting point for the material that we used to compile our reference corpus.

The idea of using this database as a grammar checker is to analyse an input text and detect any sequence of words that cannot be found in the n-gram database (which only contains n-grams with frequency equal to or greater than 40) and, eventually, to replace a unit in the text with one that makes a frequent n-gram. More specifically, we conduct four types of operations: accepting a text and spotting possible errors; inflecting a lemma into the appropriate form in a given context; filling-in the blanks in a text; and selecting, from a number of options, the most probable word form for a given context. In order to evaluate the algorithm, we applied it to solve exercises from a Spanish grammar book and also tested the detection of errors in a corpus of real errors made by second language learners.

The paper is organised as follows: we first offer a brief description of related work, and then explain our methodology for each of the experiments. In the next section, we show the evaluation of the results in comparison to the Microsoft Word grammar checker and, finally, we draw some conclusions and discuss lines of future work.

2 Related Work

Rule-based grammar checking started in the 1980s and crystallised in the implementation of different tools: papers by MacDonald (1983), Heidorn et al. (1982) or Richardson and Braden-Harder (1988) describe some of them (see Leacock et al., 2010, for a state of the art related to studies focused on language learning). This approach has continued to be used until recently (see Arppe, 2000; Johannessen et al., 2002; and many others) and is the basis of the work related with the popular grammar checker in Microsoft Word (different aspects of the tool are described in Dolan et al., 1993; Jensen et al., 1993; Gamon et al., 1997 and Heidorn, 2000: 181-207, among others). The knowledge-rich approach needs mechanisms to take into account errors within a rigid system of rules, and thus different strategies were implemented to gain flexibility (Weischedel and Black, 1980; Douglas and Dale, 1992; Schneider and McCoy, 1998 and others). Bolt (1992) and Kohut and Gorman (1995) evaluated several grammar checkers available at the time and concluded that, in general, none of the proposed strategies achieved high percentages of success.

There are reasons to believe that the limitations of rule-based methods could be overcome with statistical or knowledge-poor approaches, which started to be used for natural language processing in the late 1980s and 1990s. Atwell (1987) was among the first to use a statistical and knowledge-poor approach to detect grammatical errors in POS-tagging. Other studies, such as those by Knight and Chandler (1994) or Han et al. (2006), for instance, proved more successful than rule-based systems in the task of detecting article-related errors. There are also other studies (Yarowsky, 1994; Golding, 1995 or Golding and Roth, 1996) that report the application of decision lists and Bayesian classifiers for spell checking; however, these models cannot be applied to grammar error detection. Burstein et al. (2004) present an idea similar to the present paper, since they use n-grams for grammar checking. In their case, however, the model is much more complicated since it uses a machine learning approach trained on a corpus of correct English and using POS-tags bigrams as features apart from word bigrams. In addition, they use a series of statistical association measures instead of using plain frequency.

Other proposals of a similar nature are those which use the web as a corpus (Moré et al., 2004; Yin et al., 2008; Whitelaw et al., 2009), although the majority of these authors also apply different degrees of processing of the input text, such as lemmatisation, POS-tagging and chunking. Whitelaw et al. (2009), working on spell checking, are among the few who disregard explicit linguistic knowledge. Sjöbergh (2009) attempted a similar approach for grammar checking in Swedish, but with modest results. Nazar (in press) reports on an experiment where corpus statistics are used to solve a German-language multiple choice exam, the result being a score similar to that of a native speaker. The system does not use any kind of explicit knowledge of German grammar or vocabulary: answers are found by simply querying a search engine and selecting the most frequent combination of words. The present paper is a continuation and extension of that idea, now with a specific application to the practical problem of checking the grammar of texts in Spanish.

In spite of decades of work on the subject of grammar-checking algorithms, as summarised in the previous lines, the general experience with commercial grammar checkers is still disappointing, the most serious problem being that in the vast majority of cases errors in the analysed texts are left undetected. We believe that, in this context, a very simple grammar checker based on corpus statistics could prove to be helpful, at least as a complement to the standard procedures.

3 Methodology

In essence, the idea for this experiment is rather simple. In all the operations, we contrast the sequences of words as they are found in an input text with those recorded in Google's database. In the error detection phase, the algorithm will flag as an error any sequence of two words that is not found in the database, unless either of the two words is not found individually in the database, in which case the sequence is ignored. The idea is that in a correction phase the algorithm will output a ranked list of suggestions to replace each detected error in order to make the text match the n-grams of the database. The following subsections offer a detailed description of the methodology of each experiment. For the evaluation, we tested whether the algorithm could solve grammar exercises from a text-book (Montolío, 2000), which is one of the most widely used Spanish text-books for academic writing for native speakers, covering various topics such as pronouns, determiners, prepositions, verb tenses, and so on. In addition, for error detection we used a corpus of L2 learners (Lozano, 2009).

3.1 Error Detection

Error detection is, logically, the first phase of a grammar checking algorithm and, in practice, would be followed by some correction operation, such as those described in 3.2 to 3.4. In the error detection procedure, the algorithm accepts an input sentence or text and retrieves the frequency of all word types (of forms as they appear in the text and not the lemmata) as well as all the different bigrams as sequences of word forms, excluding punctuation signs. The output of this process is the same text with two different types of flags indicating, on the one hand, that a particular word is not found or is not frequent enough and, on the other hand, that a bigram is not frequent. The frequency threshold can be an arbitrary parameter, which would measure the "sensitivity" of the grammar checker. As already mentioned, the minimum frequency of Google n-grams is 40.

As the corpus is very large, there are a large number of proper nouns, even names that are unusual in Spanish. For example, in the sentence *En 1988 Jack Nicholson, Helen Hunt y Kim Basinger recibieron sendos Oscar* ('In 1988 Jack Nicholson, Helen Hunt and Kim Basinger each received one Oscar'), bigrams such as *y Kim* or, of course, others like *Jack Nicholson* are considered frequent by the system because these actors are famous in the Spanish context, but this is not the case for the bigram *Martín Fiz*, belonging to another sentence, which is considered infrequent and treated as an error (false positive), because the name of this Spanish athlete does not appear with sufficient frequency. Future versions will address this issue.

3.2 Multiple Choice Exercises

In this scenario, the algorithm is fed with a sentence or text which has a missing word and a series of possibilities from which to decide the most appropriate one for that particular context.

For instance, given an input sentence such as *El coche se precipitó por *un,una* pendiente* ('The car plunged down a slope'), the algorithm has to choose the correct option between *un* and *una* (i.e., the masculine and feminine forms of the indefinite article).

Confronted with this input data, the algorithm composes different trigrams with each possibility and one word immediately to the left and right of the target position. Thus, in this case, one of the trigrams would be *por un pendiente* and, similarly, the other would be *por una pendiente*. As in 3.1., the selection procedure is based on a frequency comparison of the trigrams in the n-gram database, which in this case favours the first option, which is the correct one.

In case the trigram is not found in the database,

there are two back-off operations, consisting in separating each trigram into two bigrams, with the first and second position in one case and the second and third in the other. The selected option will be the one with the two bigrams that, added together, have the highest frequency.

3.3 Inflection

In this case, the exercise consists in selecting the appropriate word form of a given lemma in a given context. Thus, for instance, in another exercise from Montolío's book, *No le *satisfacer* en absoluto el acuerdo al que llegaron con sus socios alemanes* ('[He/She] is not at all satisfied with the agreement reached with [his/her] German partners'), the algorithm has to select the correct verbal inflection of the lemma *satisfacer*.

This operation is similar to the previous one, the only difference being that in this case we use a lexical database of Spanish that allows us to obtain all the inflected forms of a given lemma. In this case, then, the algorithm searches for the trigram *le * en*, where * is defined as all the inflectional paradigm of the lemma.

3.4 Fill-in the blanks

The operation of filling-in the blank spaces in a sentence is another typical grammar exercise. In this case, the algorithm accepts an input sentence such as *Los asuntos * más preocupan a la sociedad son los relacionados con la economía* ('The issues of greatest concern to society are those related to the economy'), from the same source, and suggests a list of candidates. As in the previous cases, the algorithm will search for a trigram such as *asuntos * más*, where the * wildcard in this case means any word, or more precisely, the most frequent word in that position. In the case of the previous example, which is an exercise about relative pronouns, the most frequent word in the corpus and the correct option is *que*.

4 Results and Evaluation

4.1 Result of error detection

The results of our experiments are summarised in Table 1, where we distinguish between different types of grammar errors and correction operations. The table also offers a comparison of the performance of the algorithm against Microsoft Word 2007 with the same dataset. In the first column of the table we divide the errors into different types as classified in Montolío's book. Performance figures are represented as usual in information retrieval (for details, see Manning et al., 2008): the columns represent the numbers of true positives (tp), which are those errors that were effectively detected by each system; false negatives (fn) referring to errors that were not detected, and false positives (fp), consisting in those cases that were correct, but which the system wrongly flagged as errors. These values allowed us to define precision (P) as $tp/(tp+fp)$, recall (R) as $tp/(tp+fn)$ and $F1$ as $2.P.R/(P+R)$.

The algorithm detects (with a success rate of 80.59%), for example, verbs with an incorrect morphology, such as **apreto* (instead of *aprieto*, 'I press'). Nevertheless, the system also makes more interesting detections, such as the incorrect selection of the verb tense, which requires information provided by the context: *Si os vuelve a molestar, no *volved a hablar con él* ('If [he] bothers you again, do not talk to him again'). In this sentence, the correct tense for the second verb is *volváis*, as the imperative in negative sentences is made with the subjunctive. In the same way, it is possible to detect incorrect uses of the adjective *sendos* ('for each other'), which cannot be put after the noun, among other particular constraints: combinations such as **los sendos actores* ('both actors') or **han cerrado filiales sendas* ('they have closed both subsidiaries') are marked as incorrect by the system.

In order to try to balance the bias inherent to a grammar text-book, we decided to replicate the experiment with real errors. The decision to extract exercises from a grammar book was based on the idea that this book would contain a diverse sample of the most typical mistakes, and in this sense it is representative. But as the examples given by the authors are invented, they are often uncommon and unnatural, and of course this frequently has a negative effect on performance. We thus repeated the experiment using sentences from the CEDEL2 corpus (Lozano, 2009), which is a corpus of essays in Spanish written by non-native speakers with different levels of proficiency.

For this experiment, we only used essays written by students classified as "very advanced". We extracted 65 sentences, each containing one error.

	This Experiment						Word 2007					
Type of error	**tp**	**fn**	**fp**	**% P**	**% R**	**% F1**	**tp**	**fn**	**fp**	**% P**	**% R**	**% F1**
gerund	9	8	9	50	52.94	51.42	9	8	1	**90**	52.94	**66.66**
verb morphology	54	17	13	80.59	76.05	78.25	60	11	3	**95.23**	**84.50**	**89.54**
numerals	4	9	7	36.36	30.76	33.32	6	7	0	**100**	**46.15**	**63.15**
grammatical number	10	8	1	90.90	55.55	68.95	10	8	1	90.90	55.55	68.95
prepositions	25	40	17	59.52	**38.46**	**46.72**	13	52	0	**100**	20	33.33
adjective "sendos"	5	0	1	83.33	**100**	**90.90**	1	4	0	**100**	20	33.33
various	55	52	52	51.40	**51.40**	**51.40**	33	74	10	**76.74**	30.84	43.99
total	162	134	100	61.83	**54.72**	58.05	132	164	15	**89.79**	44.59	**59.58**

Table 1: Summary of the results obtained by our algorithm in comparison to Word 2007

Since the idea was to check grammar, we only selected material that was orthographically correct, any minor typos being corrected beforehand. In comparison with the mistakes dealt with in the grammar book, the kind of grammatical problems that students make are of course very different. The most frequent type of errors in this sample were gender agreement (typical in students with English as L1), lexical errors, prepositions and others such as problems with pronouns or with transitive verbs, among others.

Results of this second experiment are summarised in Table 2. Again, we compare performance against Word 2007 on the same dataset. In the case of this experiment, lexical errors and gender agreement show the best performance because these phenomena appear at the bigram level, as in **Después del boda* ('after the wedding') which should be feminine (*de la boda*), or **una tranvía eléctrica* ('electric tram') which should be masculine (*un tranvía*). But there are other cases where the error involves elements that are separated from each other by long distances and of course will not be solved with the type of strategy we are discussing, as in the case of **un país donde el estilo de vida es avanzada* ('a country with an advanced lifestyle'), where the adjective *avanzada* is wrongly put in feminine when it should be masculine (*avanzado*), because it modifies a masculine noun *estilo*.

In general, results of the detection phase are far from perfect but at least comparable to those achieved by Word in these categories. The main difference between the performance of the two algorithms is that ours tends to flag a much larger number of errors, incurring in many false positives and severely degrading performance. The behaviour of Word is the opposite, it tends to flag fewer errors, thus leaving many errors undetected. It can be argued that, in a task like this, it is preferable to have false positives rather than false negatives, because the difficult part of producing a text is to find the errors. However, a system that produces many false positives will lose the confidence of the user. In any case, more important than a difference in precision is the fact that both systems tend to detect very different types of errors, which reinforces the idea that statistical algorithms could be a useful complement to a rule-based system.

4.2 Result of multiple choice exercise

The results of the multiple choice exercise in the book are shown in Table 3. Again, we compared performance with that achieved by Word. In order to make this program solve a multiple choice exercise we submitted the different possibilities for each sentence and checked whether it was able to detect errors in the wrong sentences and leave the correct ones unflagged.

Results in this case are similar in general to those reported in Section 4.1. An example of a correct trial is with the fragment **el,la* génesis del problema* ('the genesis of the problem'), where the option selected by the algorithm is *la génesis* (feminine gender). In contrast, it is not capable of giving the correct answer when the context is very general, such as in **los,las* pendientes son uno de los complementos más vendidos como regalo* ('Earrings are one of the accessories most frequently sold as a gift'), in which the words to choose from are at the beginning of the sentence and they are followed by *son* ('they are'), which comes from *ser*, perhaps the most frequent and polysemous Spanish verb. The correct answer is *los* (masculine article), but the system offers the incorrect *las* (feminine) because of the polysemy of the word, since *las pendientes* also exist, but means 'the slopes' or even 'the ones pending'.

	This Experiment						Word 2007					
Type of error	**tp**	**fn**	**fp**	**% P**	**% R**	**% F1**	**tp**	**fn**	**fp**	**% P**	**% R**	**% F1**
gender agreement	9	6	3	75	**60**	**66.66**	7	8	0	**100**	46.66	63.63
lexical selection	16	10	4	80	**61.53**	**69.56**	4	22	0	**100**	15.38	26.66
prepositions	2	11	2	**50**	**15.38**	**23.52**	0	13	0	0	0	0
various	4	7	5	44.44	**36.36**	**39.99**	3	8	3	**50**	27.27	35.29
total	31	34	17	64.58	**47.69**	**54.86**	14	51	3	**82.35**	21.53	34.14

Table 2: Replication of the experiment with a corpus of non-native speakers (CEDEL2, Lozano, 2009)

	Trials	This Experiment		Word 2007	
Type of error		**Correct**	**% P**	**Correct**	**% P**
adverbs	9	8	**88.89**	5	55.55
genre	10	7	**70.00**	3	30
confusion DO-IO	4	2	50.00	2	50

Table 3: Solution of the multiple choice exercise

4.3 Result of inflection exercise

Results in the case of the inflection exercise are summarised in Table 4. When giving verb forms, results are correct in 66.67% of the cases. For instance, in the case of *La mayoría de la gente *creer* que...* ('The majority of people think that...'), the correct answer is *cree*, among other possibilities such as *creen* (plural) or *creía* (past). But results are generally unsuccessful (22.22%) when choosing the correct tense, such as in the case of *Si el problema me *atañer* a mí, ya hubiera hecho algo para remediarlo* ('If the problem was of my concern, I would have already done something to solve it'). In this example, the correct verb tense is *atañera* or *atañese*, both of which are forms for the third person past subjunctive used in conditional clauses, but the system gives *atañe*, a correct form for the verb *atañer* that, nevertheless, cannot be used in this sentence. As it can be seen, the problem is extremely difficult for a statistical procedure (there are around 60 verb forms in Spanish), and this may explain why the results of this type of exercise were more disappointing.

Type of error	Trials	Correct	% P
verb number	9	6	66.67
verb tense	9	2	22.22

Table 4: Results of the inflection exercise

4.4 Result of filling-in the blanks

When asked to restore a missing word in a sentence, the algorithm is capable of offering the correct answer in cases such as *El abogado * defendió al peligroso asesino...* ('The lawyer -who- defended the dangerous murderer...'), where the missing word is *que*. Other cases were not solved correctly, as the fragment ** ácida manzana* ('the acid apple'), because the bigram *la ácida* is much less frequent than *lluvia ácida*, 'acid rain', the wrong candidate proposed by the system. Results of this exercise are summarised in Table 5.

Type of error	Trials	Correct	% P
articles	7	4	57.14
pronouns	7	3	42.86

Table 5: Results of the fill-in-the-blank exercise

5 Conclusions and Future Work

In the previous sections we have outlined a first experiment in the detection of different types of grammar errors. In summary, the algorithm is able to detect difficult mistakes such as **informes conteniendo* (instead of *informes que contenían* 'reports that contained': a wrong use of the gerund) or **máscaras antigases* (instead of *máscaras antigás* 'gas masks', an irregular plural), which are errors that were not detected by MS Word.

One of the difficulties we found is that, despite the fact that the corpus used is probably the most extensive corpus ever compiled, there are bigrams that are not present in it. This is not surprising, since one of the functions of linguistic competence is the capacity to represent and make comprehensible strings of words which have never been produced before. Another problem is that frequency is not always useful for detecting mistakes, because the norm can be very separated from real use. An example of this is that, in one of the error detection exercises, the system considers that the participle *freídos* ('fried') is incorrect because it is not in the corpus, but the participle is actually correct, even when the majority of speakers think that only the irregular form (*frito*) is normative. The opposite is also true: some incorrect structures are very frequently used and many speakers perceive them as correct, such as *ayer noche* instead of *ayer por la noche* ('last night'), or some very common Gallicisms such as **medidas a tomar* instead of *medidas por tomar* 'measures to be taken', or **asunto a discutir* ('matter to discuss') which should be *asunto para discutir*.

Several ideas have been put forward to address these difficulties in future improvements to this research, such as the use of trigrams and longer *n*-grams instead of only bigrams for error detection. POS-tagging and proper noun detection are also essential. Another possibility is to complement the corpus with different Spanish corpora, including press articles and other sources. We are also planning to repeat the experiment with a new version of the *n*-gram database this time not as plain word forms but as classes of objects such that the corpus will have greater power of generalisation. Following another line of research that we have already started (Nazar and Renau, in preparation), we will produce clusters of words according to their distributional similarity, which will result in a sort of Spanish taxonomy. This can be accomplished because all the words that represent, say, the category of vehicles are, in general, very similar as regards their distribution. Once we have organised the lexicon of the corpus into categories, we will replace those words by the name of the category they belong to, for instance, PERSON, NUMBER, VEHICLE, COUNTRY, ORGANISATION, BEVERAGE, ANIMAL, PLANT and so on. By doing this, the Google *n*-gram corpus will be useful to represent a much more diverse variety of *n*-grams than those it actually contains. The implications of this idea go far beyond the particular field of grammar checking and include the study of collocations and of predicate-argument structures in general. We could ask, for instance, which are the most typical agents of the Spanish verb *disparar* (to shoot). Searching for the trigram *los * dispararon* in the database, we can learn, for instance, that those agents can be *soldados* (soldiers), *españoles* (Spaniards), *guardias* (guards), *policías* (policemen), *cañones* (cannons), *militares* (the military), *ingleses* (the British), *indios* (indians) and so on. Such a line of study could produce interesting results and greatly improve the rate of success of our grammar checker.

Acknowledgments

This research has been made possible thanks to funding from the Spanish Ministry of Science and Innovation, project: "Agrupación semántica y relaciones lexicológicas en el diccionario", lead researcher J. DeCesaris (HUM2009-07588/FILO); APLE: "Procesos de actualización del léxico del español a partir de la prensa", 2010-2012, lead researcher: M. T. Cabré (FFI2009-12188-C05-01/FILO) and Fundación Comillas in relation with the project "Diccionario de aprendizaje del español como lengua extranjera". The authors would like to thank the anonymous reviewers for their helpful comments, Cristóbal Lozano for providing the non-native speaker corpus CEDEL2, Mark Andrews for proofreading, the team of the CIBER HPC Platform of Universitat Pompeu Fabra (Silvina Re and Milton Hoz) and the people that compiled and decided to share the Google Books *N*-gram corpus with the rest of the community (Michel et al., 2010).

References

Antti Arppe. 2000. Developing a Grammar Checker for Swedish. *Proceedings of the Twelfth Nordic Conference in Computational Linguistics. Trondheim, Norway*, pp. 5–77.

Eric Steven Atwell. 1987. How to Detect Grammatical Errors in a Text without Parsing it. *Proceedings of the Third Conference of the European Association for Computational Linguistics, Copenhagen, Denmark*, pp. 38–45.

Philip Bolt. 1992. An Evaluation of Grammar-Checking Programs as Self-help Learning Aids for Learners of English as a Foreign Language. *Computer Assisted Language Learning*, 5(1):49–91.

Jill Burstein, Martin Chodorow, Claudia Leacock. 2004. Automated Essay Evaluation: the Criterion Writing Service. *AI Magazine*, 25(3):27–36.

William B. Dolan, Lucy Vanderwende, Stephen D. Richardson. 1993. Automatically Deriving Structured Knowledge Base from On-Line Dictionaries. *Proceedings of the Pacific ACL. Vancouver, BC.*

Shona Douglas, Robert Dale. 1992. Towards robust PATR. *Proceedings of the 15th International Conference on Computational Linguistics, Nantes*, pp. 468–474.

Michael Gamon, Carmen Lozano, Jessie Pinkham, Tom Reutter. 1997. Practical Experience with Grammar Sharing in Multilingual NLP. *Proceedings of the Workshop on Making NLP Work. ACL Conference, Madrid.*

Andrew Golding. 1995. A Bayesian Hybrid Method for Context Sensitive Spelling Correction. *Proceedings of the Third Workshop on Very Large Corpora*, pp. 39–53.

Andrew Golding, Dan Roth. 1996. Applying Winnow to Context Sensitive Spelling Correction. *Proceedings of the International Conference on Machine Learning*, pp. 182–190.

Na-Rae Han, Martin Chodorow, Claudia Leacock. 2006. Detecting Errors in English Article Usage by non-Native Speakers. *Natural Language Engineering*, 12(2), pp. 115–129.

George E. Heidorn. 2000. Intelligent writing assistance. *In Dale, R, Moisl H, Somers H, eds. Handbook of Natural Language Processing: Techniques and Applications for the Processing of Language as Text. New York: Marcel Dekker.*

George E. Heidorn, Karen Jensen, Lance A. Miller, Roy J. Byrd, Martin Chodorow. 1982. The EPISTLE text-critiquing system. *IBM Systems Journal*, 21, pp. 305–326.

Karen Jensen, George E. Heidorn, Stephen Richardson, eds. 1993. *Natural Language Processing: The PNLP Approach.* Kluwer Academic Publishers.

Jane Bondi Johannessen, Kristin Hagen, Pia Lane. 2002. The Performance of a Grammar Checker with Deviant Language Input. *Proceedings of the 19th International Conference on Computational Linguistics. Taipei, Taiwan*, pp. 1–8.

Kevin Knight, Ishwar Chandler. 1994. Automated Postediting of Documents. *Proceedings of National Conference on Artificial Intelligence, Seattle, USA*, pp. 779–784.

Gary F. Kohut, Kevin J. Gorman. 1995. The Effectiveness of Leading Grammar/Style Software Packages in Analyzing Business Students' Writing. *Journal of Business and Technical Communication*, 9:341–361.

Claudia Leacock, Martin Chodorow, Michael Gamon, Joel Tetreault. 2010. *Automated Grammatical Error Detection for Language Learners.* USA: Morgal and Claypool.

Cristóbal Lozano. 2009. CEDEL2: Corpus Escrito del Español L2. *In: Bretones Callejas, Carmen M. et al. (eds) Applied Linguistics Now: Understanding Language and Mind. Almería: Universidad de Almería. Almería*, pp. 197–212.

Nina H. Macdonald. 1983. The UNIX Writer's Workbench Software: Rationale and Design. *Bell System Technical Journal*, 62, pp. 1891–1908.

Chistopher D. Manning, Prabhakar Raghavan, Hinrich Schütze. 2008. *Introduction to Information Retrieval.* Cambridge University Press.

Jean-Baptiste Michel, Yuan Kui Shen, Aviva Presser Aiden, Adrian Veres, Matthew K. Gray, The Google Books Team, Joseph P. Pickett, Dale Hoiberg, Dan Clancy, Peter Norvig, Jon Orwant, Steven Pinker, Martin A. Nowak, Erez Lieberman Aiden. 2011. Quantitative Analysis of Culture Using Millions of Digitized Books. *Science* 331(6014), pp. 176–182.

Estrella Montolío, ed. 2000. *Manual práctico de escritura académica.* Barcelona: Ariel.

Joaquim Moré, Salvador Climent, Antoni Oliver. 2004. A Grammar and Style Checker Based on Internet Searches. *Proceedings of LREC 2004, Lisbon, Portugal.*

Rogelio Nazar. In press. Algorithm qualifies for C1 courses in German exam without previous knowledge of the language: an example of how corpus linguistics can be a new paradigm in Artificial Intelligence. *Proceedings of Corpus Linguistics Conference, Birmingham, 20-22 July 2011.*

Rogelio Nazar, Irene Renau. In preparation. A co-ocurrence taxonomy from a general language corpus. *Proceedings of the 15th EURALEX International Congress, Oslo, 7-11 August 2012.*

Stephen Richardson, Lisa Braden-Harder. 1988. The Experience of Developing a Large-Scale Natural Language Text Processing System: CRITIQUE. *Proceedings of the Second Conference on Applied Natural Language Processing (ANLC '88). ACL, Stroudsburg, PA, USA*, pp. 195–202.

David Schneider, Kathleen McCoy. 1998. Recognizing Syntactic Errors in the Writing of Second Language Learners. *Proceedings of the 36th Annual Meeting of the ACL and 17th International Conference on Computational Linguistics, Montreal, Canada*, pp. 1198–1204.

Jonas Sjöbergh. 2009. *The Internet as a Normative Corpus: Grammar Checking with a Search Engine.* Techical Report, Dept. of Theoretical Computer Science, Kungliga Tekniska Högskolan.

Ralph M. Weischedel, John Black. 1980. Responding-to potentially unparseable sentences. *American Journal of Computational Linguistics*, 6:97–109.

Casey Whitelaw, Ben Hutchinson, Grace Y. Chung, Gerard Ellis. 2009. Using the Web for Language Independent Spell Checking and Autocorrection. *Proceedings of the 2009 Conference on Empirical Methods in Natural Language Processing, Singapore*, pp. 890–899.

David Yarowsky. 1994 Decision Lists for Lexical Ambiguity Resolution: Application to Accent Restoration in Spanish and French. *Proceedings of the ACL Conference*, pp. 88–95.

Xing Yin, Jiangfeng Gao, William B. Dolan. 2008. A Web-based English Proofing System for English as a Second Language Users. *Proceedings of the 3rd International Joint Conference on Natural Language Processing, Hyderabad, India*, pp. 619–624.

LELIE: A Tool Dedicated to Procedure and Requirement Authoring

Flore Barcellini, Corinne Grosse
CNAM, 41 Rue Gay Lussac,
Paris, France,
Flore.Barcellini@cnam.fr

Camille Albert, Patrick Saint-Dizier
IRIT-CNRS, 118 route de Narbonne,
31062 Toulouse cedex France
stdizier@irit.fr

Abstract

This short paper relates the main features of LELIE, phase 1, which detects errors made by technical writers when producing procedures or requirements. This results from ergonomic observations of technical writers in various companies.

1 Objectives

The main goal of the LELIE project is to produce an analysis and a piece of software based on language processing and artificial intelligence that detects and analyses potential risks of different kinds (first health and ecological, but also social and economical) in technical documents. We concentrate on procedural documents and on requirements (Hull et al. 2011) which are, by large, the main types of technical documents used in companies.

Given a set of procedures (e.g., production launch, maintenance) over a certain domain produced by a company, and possibly given some domain knowledge (ontology, terminology, lexical), the goal is to process these procedures and to annotate them wherever potential risks are identified. Procedure authors are then invited to revise these documents. Similarly, requirements, in particular those related to safety, often exhibit complex structures (e.g., public regulations, to cite the worse case): several embedded conditions, negation, pronouns, etc., which make their use difficult, especially in emergency situations. Indeed, procedures as well as safety requirements are dedicated to action: little space should be left to personal interpretations.

Risk analysis and prevention in LELIE is based on three levels of analysis, each of them potentially leading to errors made by operators in action:

1. Detection of inappropriate ways of writing: complex expressions, implicit elements, complex references, scoping difficulties (connectors, conditionals), inappropriate granularity level, involving lexical, semantic and pragmatic levels, inappropriate domain style,

2. Detection of domain incoherencies in procedures: detection of unusual ways of realizing an action (e.g., unusual instrument, equipment, product, unusual value such as temperature, length of treatment, etc.) with respect to similar actions in other procedures or to data extracted from technical documents,

3. Confrontation of domain safety requirements with procedures to check if the required safety constraints are met.

Most industrial areas have now defined authoring recommendations on the way to elaborate, structure and write procedures of various kinds. However, our experience with technical writers shows that those recommendations are not very strictly followed in most situations. Our objective is to develop a tool that checks ill-formed structures with respect to these recommendations and general style considerations in procedures and requirements when they are written.

In addition, authoring guidelines do not specify all the aspects of document authoring: our investigations on author practices have indeed identified a number of recurrent errors which are linguistic or conceptual which are usually not specified in authoring guidelines. These errors are basically identified from the comprehension difficulties encountered by technicians in operation using these documents to realize a task or from technical writers themselves which are aware of the errors they should avoid.

Proceedings of the EACL 2012 Workshop on Computational Linguistics and Writing, pages 35–38,
Avignon, France, April 23, 2012. ©2012 Association for Computational Linguistics

2 The Situation and our contribution

Risk management and prevention is now a major issue. It is developed at several levels, in particular via probabilistic analysis of risks in complex situations (e.g., oil storage in natural caves). Detecting potential risks by analyzing business errors on written documents is a relatively new approach. It requires the taking into account of most of the levels of language: lexical, grammatical and style and discourse.

Authoring tools for simplified language are not a new concept; one of the first checkers was developed at Boeing[1], initially for their own simplifyed English and later adapted for the ASD Simplified Technical English Specification[2]. A more recent language checking system is Acrolinx IQ by Acrolinx[3]. Some technical writing environments also include language checking functionality, e.g., MadPak[4]. Ament (2002) and Weiss (2000) developed a number of useful methodological elements for authoring technical documents and error identification and correction.

The originality of our approach is as follows. Authoring recommendations are made flexible and context-dependent, for example if negation is not allowed in instructions in general, there are, however, cases where it cannot be avoided because the positive counterpart cannot so easily be formulated, e.g., *do not dispose of the acid in the sewer*. Similarly, references may be allowed if the referent is close and non-ambiguous. However, this requires some knowledge.

Following observations in cognitive ergonomics in the project, a specific effort is realized concerning the well-formedness (following grammatical and cognitive standards) of discourse structures and their regularity over entire documents (e.g., instruction or enumerations all written in the same way).

The production of procedures includes some controls on contents, in particular action verb arguments, as indicated in the second objective above, via the Arias domain knowledge base, e.g., avoiding typos or confusions among syntactically and semantically well-identified entities such as instruments, products, equipments, values, etc.

There exists no real requirement analysis system based on language that can check the quality and the consistency of large sets of authoring recommendations. The main products are IBM Doors and Doors Trek[5], Objecteering[6], and Reqtify[7], which are essentially textual databases with advanced visual and design interfaces, query facilities for retrieving specific requirements, and some traceability functions carried out via predefined attributes. These three products also include a formal language (essentially based on attribute-value pairs) that is used to check some simple forms of coherence among large sets of requirements.

The authoring tool includes facilities for French-speaking authors who need to write in English, supporting typical errors they make via 'language transfer' (Garnier, 2011). We will not address this point here.

This project, LELIE, is based on the TextCoop system (Saint-Dizier, 2012), a system dedicated to language analysis, in particular discourse (including the taking into account of long-distance dependencies). This project also includes the Arias action knowledge base that stores prototypical actions in context, and can update them. It also includes an ASP (Answer Set Programming) solver [8] to check for various forms of incoherence and incompleteness. The kernel of the system is written in SWI Prolog, with interfaces in Java. The project is currently realized for French, an English version is under development.

The system is based on the following principles. First, the system is parameterized: the technical writer may choose the error types he wants to be checked, and the severity level for each error type when there are several such levels (e.g., there are several levels of severity associated with fuzzy terms which indeed show several levels of fuzziness). Second, the system simply tags elements identified as errors, the correction is left to the author. However, some help or guidelines are offered. For example, guidelines for reformulating a negative sentence into a positive one are proposed. Third, the way errors are displayed can be customized to the writer's habits.

We present below a kernel system that deals

[1] `http://www.boeing.com/phantom/sechecker/`

[2] ASD-STE100, `http://www.asd-ste100.org/`

[3] `http://www.acrolinx.com/`

[4] `http://www.madcapsoftware.com/products/madpak/`

[5] `http://www.ibm.com/software/awdtools/doors/`

[6] `http://www.objecteering.com/`

[7] `http://www.geensoft.com/`

[8] For an overview of ASP see Brewka et al. (2011).

with the most frequent and common errors made by technical writers independently of the technical domain. This kernel needs an in-depth customization to the domain at stake. For example, the verbs used or the terminological preferences must be implemented for each industrial context. Our system offers the control operations, but these need to be associated with domain data.

Finally, to avoid the variability of document formats, the system input is an abstract document with a minimal number of XML tags as required by the error detection rules. Managing and transforming the original text formats into this abstract format is not dealt with here.

3 Categorizing language and conceptual errors found in technical documents

In spite of several levels of human proofreading and validation, it turns out that texts still contain a large number of situations where recommendations are not followed. Reasons are analyzed in e.g. e.g., (Béguin, 2003), (Mollo et al., 2004, 2008).

Via ergonomics analysis of the activity of technical writers, we have identified several layers of recurrent error types, which are not in general treated by standard text editors such as Word or Visio, the favorite editors for procedures.

Here is a list of categories of errors we have identified. Some errors are relevant for a whole document, whereas others must only be detected in precise constructions (e.g., in instructions, which are the most constrained constructions):

- General layout of the document: size of sentences, paragraphs, and of the various forms of enumerations, homogeneity of typography, structure of titles, presence of expected structures such as summary, but also text global organization following style recommendations (expressed in TextCoop via a grammar), etc.
- Morphology: in general passive constructions and future tenses must be avoided in instructions.
- Lexical aspects: fuzzy terms, inappropriate terms such as deverbals, light verb constructions or modals in instructions, detection of terms which cannot be associated, in particular via conjunctions. This requires typing lexical data.
- Grammatical complexity: the system checks for various forms of negation, referential forms, sequences of conditional expressions, long sequences of coordination, complex noun complements, and relative clause embeddings. All these constructions often make documents difficult to understand.
- Uniformity of style over a set of instructions, over titles and various lists of equipments, uniformity of expression of safety warnings and advice.
- Correct position in the document of specific fields: safety precautions, prerequisites, etc.
- Structure completeness, in particular completeness of case enumerations with respect to to known data, completeness of equipment enumerations, via the Arias action base.
- Regular form of requirements: context of application properly written (e.g., via conditions) followed by a set of instructions.
- Incorrect domain value, as detected by Arias.

When a text is analyzed, the system annotates the original document (which is in our current implementation a plain text, a Word or an XML document): revisions are only made by technical writers.

Besides tags which must be as explicit as possible, colors indicate the severity level for the error considered (the same error, e.g., use of fuzzy term, can have several severity levels). The most severe errors must be corrected first. At the moment, we propose four levels of severity:

ERROR Must be corrected.

AVOID Preferably avoid this usage, think about an alternative,

CHECK this is not really bad, but it is recommended to make sure this is clear; this is also used to make sure that argument values are correct, when a non-standard one is found.

ADVICE Possibly not the best language realization, but this is probably a minor problem. It is not clear whether there are alternatives.

The model, the implementation and the results are presented in detail in (Barcellini et al., 2012).

4 Perspectives

We have developed the first phase of the LELIE project: detecting authoring errors in technical documents that may lead to risks. We identified a number of errors: lexical, business, grammatical, and stylistic. Errors have been identified from ergonomics investigations. The system is now fully implemented on the TextCoop platform and has been evaluated on a number of documents. It is now of much interest to evaluate user's reactions.

We have implemented the system kernel. The main challenge ahead of us is the customization to a given industrial context. This includes:

- Accurately testing the system on the company's documents so as to filter out a few remaining odd error detections,
- Introducing the domain knowledge via the domain ontology and terminology, and enhancing the rules we have developed to take every aspect into account,
- Analyzing and incorporating into the system the authoring guidelines proper to the company that may have an impact on understanding and therefore on the emergence of risks,
- Implementing the interfaces between the original user documents and our system, with the abstract intermediate representation we have defined,
- Customizing the tags expressing errors to the users profiles and expectations, and enhancing correction schemas.

When sufficiently operational, the kernel of the system will be made available on line, and probably the code will be available in open-source mode or via a free or low cost license.

Acknowledgements

This project is funded by the French National Research Agency ANR. We also thanks reviewers and the companies that showed a strong interest in our project, let us access to their technical documents and allowed us to observed their technical writers.

References

Kurt Ament. 2002. *Single Sourcing. Building modular documentation*, W. Andrew Pub.

Flore Barcellini, Camille Albert, Corinne Grosse, Patrick Saint-Dizier. 2012. *Risk Analysis and Prevention: LELIE, a Tool dedicated to Procedure and Requirement Authoring,* LREC 2012, Istanbul.

Patrice Béguin. 2003. Design as a mutual learning process between users and designers, *Interacting with computers*, 15 (6).

Sarah Bourse, Patrick Saint-Dizier. 2012. *A Repository of Rules and Lexical Resources for Discourse Structure Analysis: the Case of Explanation Structures*, LREC 2012, Istanbul.

Gerhard Brewka, Thomas Eiter, Mirosław Truszczyński. 2011. Answer set programming at a glance. *Communications of the ACM* 54 (12), 92–103.

Marie Garnier. 2012. Automatic correction of adverb placement errors: an innovative grammar checker system for French users of English, Eurocall'10 proceedings, Elsevier.

Walther Kintsch. 1988. *The Role of Knowledge in Discourse Comprehension: A Construction-Integration Model*, Psychological Review, vol 95-2.

Elizabeth C. Hull, Kenneth Jackson, Jeremy Dick. 2011. *Requirements Engineering*, Springer.

William C. Mann, Sandra A. Thompson. 1988. Rhetorical Structure Theory: Towards a Functional Theory of Text Organisation, *TEXT* 8 (3), 243–281. Sandra A. Thompson. (ed.), 1992. *Discourse Description: diverse linguistic analyses of a fund raising text*, John Benjamins.

Dan Marcu. 1997. *The Rhetorical Parsing of Natural Language Texts*, ACL'97.

Dan Marcu. 2000. *The Theory and Practice of Discourse Parsing and Summarization*, MIT Press.

Vanina Mollo, Pierre Falzon. 2004. *Auto and alloconfrontation as tools for reflective activities.* Applied Ergonomics, 35 (6), 531–540.

Vanina Mollo, Pierre Falzon. 2008. *The development of collective reliability: a study of therapeutic decision-making*, Theoretical Issues in Ergonomics Science, 9(3), 223–254.

Dietmar Rösner, Manfred Stede. 1992. *Customizing RST for the Automatic Production of Technical Manuals*, In Robert Dale et al. (eds.) Aspects of Automated Natural Language Generation. Berlin: Springer, 199–214.

Dietmar Rösner, Manfred Stede. 1994. *Generating multilingual technical documents from a knowledge base: The TECHDOC project*, In: Proc. of the International Conference on Computational Linguistics, COLING-94, Kyoto.

Patrick Saint-Dizier. 2012. Processing Natural Language Arguments with the TextCoop Platform, *Journal of Argumentation and Computation.*

Edmond H. Weiss. 2000. *Writing remedies. Practical exercises for technical writing*, Oryx Press.

Focus Group on Computer Tools Used for Professional Writing and Preliminary Evaluation of LinguisTech

Marie-Josée Goulet
University of Quebec in Outaouais
Gatineau, Quebec
J8X 3X7, Canada
marie-josee.goulet@uqo.ca

Annie Duplessis
University of Quebec in Outaouais
Gatineau, Quebec
J8X 3X7, Canada
dupa08@uqo.ca

Abstract

This paper focuses on computer writing tools used during the production of documents in a professional setting. Computer writing tools include language technologies, for example electronic dictionaries and text correction software, as well as information and communication technologies, for example collaborative platforms and search engines. As we will see, professional writing has become an entirely computerised activity. First, we report on a focus group with professional writers, during which they discussed their experience using computer tools to write documents. We will describe their practices, point out the most important problems they encounter, and analyse their needs. Second, we describe LinguisTech, a reference web site for language professionals (translators, writers, language instructors, etc.) that was launched in Canada in September, 2011. We comment on a preliminary evaluation that we conducted to determine if this new platform meets professional writers' needs.

1 Introduction

This paper focuses on computer writing tools used during the production of documents, be they letters, newsletters, policies, guidelines, releases or annual reports, in a professional setting, what we call *professional writing* (Beaudet, 1998). The importance of professional writing in private and public organisations is undeniable as written documents serve as communication between employees, support in decision making and organisational memory.

Computer tools can be used in a variety of writing situations, such as learning how to write in schools (Kuhn et al., 2009), learning a second language (Milton and Cheng, 2010), and helping people with cognitive, visual or motor disabilities (Majaranta and Kari-Jouko, 2002). However, our knowledge and understanding of computer tools used by professional writers are somewhat limited. Which tools are used by professional writers? Are these tools meeting their needs? Do writers know what these tools can do? Kavanagh (1999) is one of the few authors who investigated such questions. In his detailed analysis of Microsoft Word, he demonstrated that the text processor mostly meets formatting and editing needs, and that it cannot, by far, support every step of the professional writing process. Kavanagh's research was quite a revelation at the time. However, many years have passed, and we have seen few studies on that subject since then.

Writers have seen their profession evolve over the last 20 years. First, the massive use of personal computers has transformed writing practices as writers now have to cope with machines (computers, printers, scanners) and computer tools (text processors, search engines, electronic messaging systems, electronic dictionaries, spelling checkers, and collaborative platforms), whose number increases each year. Surely, this computer revolution has simplified professional writers' work as computer tools can help render more efficient document formatting, proofreading, collaborative writing, and content reusing, to name just a few examples. In that perspective, computer tools should help professional writers produce more documents. However, the number of documents that need to be produced in today's society, especially in the service sector (Nakbi, 2002), is such that productivity's expectations towards writers are

Proceedings of the EACL 2012 Workshop on Computational Linguistics and Writing, pages 39–47,
Avignon, France, April 23, 2012. ©2012 Association for Computational Linguistics

great. And, as we will discuss in this paper, computer tools are not always well-adapted to professional writing.

Also, the webification of human knowledge is creating new expectations in professional writers' skills. While only a few years ago, documents written according to printing standards were scanned and published on the web as images, an increasing number of documents are now produced according to hypertext standards. Therefore, professional writers have to master new specialised skills, for example in hypertext information organisation, document design, and computer science (Kavanagh, 2006).

The goal of this paper is twofold. First, it reports on an exploratory study on computer tools used for the production of written documents in the workplace (see Section 2). This research consisted in asking questions to professional writers during a focus group. We will present a summary of those discussions and analyse professional writers' needs in terms of computer writing tools. Second, the paper describes and analyses LinguisTech, a reference web site for language professionals that was launched in Canada in September, 2011 (see Section 3). This preliminary evaluation will allow us to determine if this new platform actually meets professional writers' needs.

2 Exploratory Study on Computer Tools Used by Professional Writers

2.1 Focus Group

A focus group was conducted with volunteers. This method is well suited for exploring subjects, gathering opinions on a specific topic, and asking questions to participants when more details are needed. Participants were met together and could interact with each other. Eight francophone professional writers working in Canada's capital region (Gatineau-Ottawa) participated in our study[1]. Our principal selection criteria was that the candidates' main task consisted in writing practical texts or, at least, that this be the most important part of their job. The participants had between 3 and 12 years of experience in professional writing and came from different sectors: government and parapublic, enterprise, non-profit organisation, professional association and print media.

Prior to the focus group, it was assumed that professional writing had become an entirely computerised activity. The main objective of the study reported in this paper was to gather information on professional writers' experience with computer tools. We also wanted to explore their thoughts on how these tools could better support professional writing in general. Here is a sample of the questions that we asked them. Those questions were addressed to the group, not to individuals.

- In your every day job as a professional writer, what computer tools do you use?
- For what specific task of the writing process do you use those tools?
- Do you exclusively use computer tools or also printed material?
- Do you think that using computer tools improve your productivity?
- Do you have any problems using those computer tools?
- How, in your opinion, could computer tools better help professional writers?
- What other computer tools would you like to use?

We organised two meetings of one and a half hour each, for a total of three hours. The meetings were recorded and transcribed, rendering a 27,000-word text. This text was analysed by identifying all relevant information on professional writers' experience with computer tools, a step we repeated until we could not find any new information.

During the focus group, we used the general expression *computer tool* to refer to any tool used to accomplish a task related to professional writing. But as we will see later, this concept includes two types of computer tools: language technologies, for example electronic dictionaries and text correction software, and information and communication technologies, for example collaborative platforms and search engines.

2.2 Analytical Framework

In order to present results from the focus group, we need a standard procedural model of the writing process. We will use Clerc's model (1998, 2000), which is based on the actual professional writers' practice. This model includes five steps: assignment analysis, information research, information structuring,

[1] As Geoffrion (1998) explains, the focus group calls for a small number of participants, preferably between six and twelve.

writing and revising. Table 1 gives an overview of the tasks accomplished at every step of the writing process.

Step 1: Assignment analysis	• Meet supervisor or client • Define mandate • Establish writing strategy and calendar • Write a proposal, if necessary
Step 2: Information research	• Establish a research strategy • Collect information
Step 3: Information structuring	• Select information • Group information • Determine information ordering • Find the main thread
Step 4: Writing	• Put plan into words • Write headings
Step 5: Revising	• Evaluate information • Evaluate structure • Evaluate writing

Table 1. Tasks done at different steps of the writing process in a professional setting (Clerc, 2000)

Although this model is in general suited for the purpose of our research, we needed to make some adjustments. First, since none of the participants seem to be using computer tools during the assignment analysis (in fact, no one brought this step up during the discussion), we excluded this step from our analysis. Second, "Information research" was renamed "Information research and processing", which better represents the fact that writers have to process (even summarily) the information during the research in order to evaluate information relevance. Third, we added the document transmission task but, instead of creating a new distinct step, we included it in the last one of the model. This step is thus renamed "Revising and document transmission". Table 2 shows a summary of the modified analytical framework.

Step 1: Information research and processing
Step 2: Information structuring
Step 3: Writing
Step 4: Revising and document transmission

Table 2. Modified analytical framework (adapted from Clerc, 2000)

2.3 Results

Results will be presented according to the four steps of our analytical framework.

Information Research and Processing

Morizio (2006) defines information research as an operation consisting of matching an information need and a document. In the context of our study, the professional writer formulates an information need after receiving an assignment from his superior or customer. As expected, most of the documents consulted by our professional writers are in electronic format: files either saved on a drive or available on a network (intranet or internet). Professional writers seem to take advantage of what the web has to offer, consulting newspapers, annual reports, web pages and social networks. Although the content of some of these web documents may be questioned (the content of a blog for example), they are still considered as "interesting" sources, which indicates the professional writers' interest and adaptability towards new forms of electronic information. However, the participants criticised the immensity of the web, which keeps growing day after day. If we add the fact that many documents found on the web are duplicated, and that the same document can be found in different format (HTML, PDF), this can really slow down the information gathering because the writer has to verify if it is in fact the same document. They do not blame the web for offering too much information, but they wish that this information be better organised and easier to find.

As we said earlier, professional writers summarily analyse documents during the information gathering, and they save relevant documents in personal folders. We identified two strategies used by writers to process the information at this stage of the writing project[2]. One of these strategies consists in searching for information within documents using the search engine available in conventional operating systems. Professional writers experience considerable difficulties with this method:

- They have to try many synonyms and lexical variants as search terms, in order to retrieve all relevant documents.
- Having copied many versions of a same document in different folders, processing the results can be a lot of work because

[2] Not all participants necessarily use both strategies.

the operating system considers copies of the same document as distinct documents.

- Still according to the participants of our study, search engines from conventional operating systems produce a lot of noise.

Those remarks are not original, but they suggest that professional writers know which computer tools, or which aspects of a particular tool, can slow down their productivity. Conventional operating systems are ubiquitous in organisations and are relatively user-friendly, so we can easily understand why our participants use them to track documents, but it appears that they are not optimal for professional writers, for whom information research and processing can be impressive in terms of workload. Of course, all writers may not classify their documents in folders astutely, a step that would allow for more specific searches afterwards in individual folders. Second, some writers may not use the advanced functions of the search engine correctly. It would be interesting in further research to study writers' behaviour in-vivo, allowing for more specific recommendations for document and information management. Also, other information management solutions should be tested in regard to professional writers' needs. Could more specialised tools improve their effectiveness, or at least their satisfaction?

The participants described a second strategy for processing information, which consists in copying and pasting parts of a source document (web page, email, PDF document, etc.) in a text file. More specifically, they create a thematic file in which they paste relevant parts of web documents, making sure that they note the source. As we know from other computational linguistics related research such as automatic summarisation by sentence extraction, this operation causes considerable information loss, making it difficult to interpret the information correctly when writing. In fact, the participants admitted that they often have to go back to the original document in order to understand the parts they had copied. In other words, professional writers need a better strategy to process textual electronic information.

The copy-and-paste method is also problematic for at least one other aspect: the manipulation of the target document. Professional writers of our study explained having problems organising the parts they copy in the target document, especially when those files contain a considerable amount of pages. Therefore, we understand why some writers chose to create a home-made database (using Excel or Access) in which they record the name of the documents they consulted and the topic(s) associated to those documents. This information can then be automatically sorted, for example, by location, topic, or name.

Information Structuring

The last task before the writing step is information structuring. This is where the writer groups chunks of information and plan the ordering. This plan is generally written using a word processor, and is sometimes created directly in the document used to write the text. Surprisingly, none of the interviewed writers use tools such as mind mapping at this stage of the writing process.

Writing

When it comes to actually writing, participants use the traditional language technologies associated with the production of professional writing, such as text correction software (Word, Antidote [3]), electronic dictionaries (Le Petit Robert, Le Grand Robert et Collins, Word Reference) and terminology data banks (Termium Plus, Le Grand dictionnaire terminologique). Professional writers use more than one language technology at once. Overall, they find these tools useful, an assessment that should reassure the language industry, which has put its focus on developing and promoting this type of tools in the past years.

Revising and Document Transmission

During the revising step, professional writers use Word's advanced functions (track changes and add comments) and the other language technologies that we already mentioned in the previous section. Regarding document transmission (or sharing), professional writers favour web-based file hosting services, even though some of them still prefer emails. We also include groupware like Google Documents in this category. As showed in Adler et al. (2006), group writing is a growing practice in professional settings, and writers in our study corroborate this evolution.

[3] As our participants write French documents, most language-specific tools that they use are for French textual data.

2.4 General Conclusions

Table 3 presents a summary of computer tools used for professional writing by the participants of the focus group.

Steps of the writing process	Computer tools used by writers
Information research and processing	• Web search engine • Email • Operating system • Office tools (text processor, database)
Information structuring	• Text processor
Writing	• Text processor • Text correction software • Dictionaries • Terminology data banks
Revising and document transmission	• Text processor (including advanced functionalities) • Text correction software • Dictionaries • Terminology data banks • File hosting service • Collaborative platform • Email

Table 3. Summary of computer tools used by professional writers of the focus group

Our study allows us to draw general conclusions on the actual practices of Canadian professional writers, or even those to come, regarding their use of computer tools. First, it confirms that professional writing has become an entirely computerised activity. In fact, except for the assignment analysis, step that our participants did not address, all tasks related to writing are accomplished using computer tools. While some tasks could still be done by hand, for example reading a document selected during information research or editing a colleague's document working in the same physical environment, this is not what professional writers choose to do. Only one participant (out of eight) mentioned using printed dictionaries, but never exclusively.

We also know, from this study, that professional writers, at least those we interviewed, would welcome the integration of additional computer tools to their workstation. In particular, they expressed the need for better information and document management software. This assessment is quite surprising considering the fact that, as Clerc (2000) notes, the information research can represent more than half of the total time dedicated to one writing project. However, although professional writers would like to use other computer tools in their work, they are afraid that they would not know how to use them.

Professional writers also wish to see other specialised tools developed. For example, the participants would use a writing memory system in contexts where they reuse content such as producing an annual report. This idea is certainly not out of reach. As a matter of fact, Allen (1999) suggested that the concept of translation memory be adapted to writing technical documents in a controlled language. A preliminary inventory confirms that such tools still exist (for example, Author-it, Congree), but we will have to verify to which extent they could be adapted to writing practical texts in general-purpose language.

Professional writers have developed specific computerised strategies for each task related to written document production, using the computer tools that were available to them. Considering all the problems mentioned by the participants, it seems that this piece-by-piece process came to saturation. From information research to document transmission, the steps leading to the production of professional documents overlap, which results in the simultaneous presence of many computer tools on the writers' workstation. At the least, the workstation presents a word processor (text that is being written, writing plan and other documents that need to be consulted), a web navigator (with many open windows or tabs), a messaging system, and language technologies. This clutter of the workstation is not without consequences. Professional writers admitted that the numerous computer manipulations that are necessary to navigate from one tool to the other slow down their work, which goes against basic ergonomics. In addition, some writers suggested that the multiplication of computer tools was interfering with their creativity. Table 4 summarises the most important problems reported by professional writers who use computer tools to produce documents.

1. Conventional operating systems are not effective to retrieve information or documents on personal computers.
2. Access to more specialised tools such as writing memory systems is difficult.
3. Desktop is cluttered up with too many computer tools and windows.
4. Training on computer tools is needed.

Table 4. Most important problems reported by professional writers who use computer tools to produce documents

In the next section, we will describe LinguisTech, a new web site dedicated to language professionals (translators, writers, language instructors, etc.), the first of its kind in Canada. We conducted a preliminary evaluation in order to determine how useful LinguisTech could be especially for professional writers.

3 Preliminary Evaluation of LinguisTech

3.1 Description of LinguisTech

LinguisTech[4] was launched in September, 2011. It is developed by the Language Technologies Research Centre (LTRC) and is funded by the Government of Canada's Canadian Language Sector Enhancement Program. LTRC describes LinguisTech as a toolbox for language professionals offering language technologies in both Canadian official languages (French and English), but also as a documentation and training centre, as well as a virtual community. We will comment more specifically on the Language Technologies Toolbox and on the Training Center, the two most developed features as of today.

LinguisTech's toolbox offers a broad selection of computer tools intended for language professionals (41 in total). The toolbox includes an inventory of free online tools useful for language-related tasks, as well as a "virtual" desktop with other information and language technologies. Computer tools included on this virtual desktop can be very expensive, but at the moment, they are available for free to Canadians who register and further obtain a password. Users can connect from any computer (Mac or PC), anywhere in the world, and access their own virtual computer. LinguisTech is also a documentation and training centre where language professionals can find, among other resources, tutorials and exercises on how to use computer tools (29 in total)[5].

Table 5 presents a complete list of computer tools, tutorials and exercises presently available in LinguisTech. Tool names in italics indicate free online tools. Tools names in grey lines indicate that a tutorial or an exercise is available, but not the tool itself.

	Tutorial or exercise available?
Office tools	
Adobe Reader X	yes
Microsoft Office	yes
Open Office	no
PDF Creator	no
Windows	yes
Search engines	
Google	yes
Library databases (uOttawa)	yes
ORBIS (uOttawa)	yes
Text correction software	
Antidote	yes
PerfectIT	no
WhiteSmoke	no
Text analysis software	
KwicKwic	no
Concept mapping tools	
CmapTools	yes
Microsoft Office Concept Mapping	yes
Text aligners	
YouAlign	yes
Concordancers	
Le Migou	yes
TextSTAT	yes
TradooIT	no
TransSearch	yes
WeBiText	yes
WordSmith Tools	yes
Dictionaries and terminology tools	
Diatopix	yes
DiCoInfo	yes
FranceTerme	no
Health Multi-Terminology Portal	no
Inspiration	no
InterActive Terminology for Europe	yes

[4] www.linguistech.ca

[5] Tutorials and exercises are developed by the Collection of Electronic Resources in Translation Technologies (CERTT) team at the University of Ottawa (see Bowker and Marshman, 2011).

Le grand dictionnaire terminologique	yes
lexicool.com	no
SDL MultiTerm 2009	no
SDL International (Trados 2007)	no
SynchroTerm	yes
Terminaute	no
TerminoWeb	no
TERMIUM Plus	yes
TermoStat Web	yes
UNTerm	no
Wiktionary	yes
WordNet	yes
Translation and localization tools	
CatsCradle	yes
Fusion Translate	no
Linguee	no
LogiTerm	yes
MultiTrans	yes
Online machine translation	yes
Reverso Promt	yes
SDL Passolo 2009	no
SDL Trados Studio 2009	no
Wordfast	no
Other resources	
Language Portal of Canada	no
Pidgin	no

Table 5. Computer tools, tutorials and exercises available in LinguisTech

3.2 Analysis

We address two research questions: How does LinguisTech respond to professional writers' needs in terms of computer tools and training material? Can LinguisTech solve any of the problems mentioned by our participants? This preliminary evaluation of LinguisTech will be presented according to the four steps of our analytical framework. The analysis is based on the information obtained from the focus group discussions (see Subsection 2.3). It is important to note that LinguisTech did not exist at the time of the focus group, which was in March, 2011, so the participants could not have used it prior to the focus group or mentioned it during the discussions.

Information Research and Processing

During information research and processing, professional writers use many computer tools: web search engines, email services, operating systems, text processors, and databases. As we can see in Table 5, LinguisTech offers many useful tools in regard to this stage of the writing process, for example Microsoft Office and Windows, many of which are accompanied by a tutorial or an exercise. Training material is also available for other tools required at this stage, for example Google search engine.

However, LinguisTech does not offer any tool, tutorial or exercise related to email, a service largely used by our participants to gather information from colleagues in the workplace. A forum where language professionals can share ideas on their profession has been recently created in LinguisTech. This forum will probably help develop a virtual community, but training material on how to effectively use this computer tool will be helpful.

Also, our participants stated that conventional operating systems are not effective to retrieve information or documents on personal computers, and that more effective information retrieval systems are needed. At the moment, LinguisTech does not provide any solution to this problem.

Information Structuring

During information structuring, our participants use a text processor, which is covered in LinguisTech, both in terms of availability and training.

Writing

While putting ideas into words, professional writers use a text processor, text correction software, some dictionaries and terminology data banks. LinguisTech offers many computer tools related to those tasks, with tutorials and exercises.

One of the problems mentioned by our participants was the difficulty to have access to specialised tools such as writing memory systems. As of today, LinguisTech does not include any specialised tools of that kind, or training material on such tools.

Revising and Document Transmission

During the last steps of the writing process, professional writers use two additional tools: file hosting services (for example Dropbox) and collaborative platforms (Google Documents). While those computer tools seem to grow in popularity among professional writers, LinguisTech does not cover them. They are neither included in the toolbox, nor is there any training material related to them.

As we reported in Subsection 2.4, the professional writers' workstation is cluttered up, meaning that the desktop is busy with many open windows. LinguisTech offers many useful computer tools, but no interface (or environment) to integrate them in an ergonomic way.

3.3 General Conclusions

In conclusion, this preliminary evaluation shows the usefulness of LinguisTech for Canadian professional writers, at least those who participated in the focus group. Most of the computer tools they use during the production of written documents are available in LinguisTech. Where LinguisTech falls short is in the integration of more effective information and document management systems and specialised writing tools (for example authoring memory systems). We do not know how many professional writers use LinguisTech[6], but we can imagine that they would expect a "reference web site for language professionals" to offer some specialised computer tools for tasks related to writing in a professional setting[7].

On the other hand, we have to admit that LinguisTech's focus on tutorials and exercises addresses concerns expressed in our exploratory study, since the absence of training on information and language technologies was one of the major problems mentioned by our participants.

Also, we think that LinguisTech could serve as an introduction to new tools, since our participants mentioned that they would welcome the integration of additional computer tools to their writing process. For example, LinguisTech includes concept mapping tools, which could be tested for information structuring, and concordancers, which could be tested for checking the correct usage of an expression during writing or revising. Those two categories of computer tools are accompanied by training material in LinguisTech.

4 Conclusion

In this paper, we presented results from a focus group with professional writers, in which they discussed their experience with computer tools used to produce documents in the workplace. As we have seen, although they would not be able to work without those tools, they reported a number of problems, namely that they do not have access to specialised writing tools, such as authoring memory systems, and that they need training on computer tools.

In the second part of the paper, we briefly described LinguisTech, a new platform for language professionals launched last September in Canada. We concluded that LinguisTech is useful for professional writers since it gives access to many computer tools intended for writing purposes, and many of those tools are accompanied by tutorials or exercises. However, according to our preliminary evaluation, LinguisTech would be even more adapted to today's professional writing if it offered more effective information and document management systems, specialised writing tools, and training material on collaborative platforms.

Acknowledgments

We would like to thank the anonymous reviewers for their useful comments and suggestions in revising this paper, and Joël Bourgeoys for his considerable help.

References

Andy Adler, John C. Nash, and Sylvie Noël. 2006. Evaluating and Implementing a Collaborative Office Document System. In Interacting with Computers, 18(4):665-682.

Jeffrey Allen. 1999. Adapting the Concept of "Translation Memory" to "Authoring Memory" for a Controlled Language Writing Environment. In Proceedings of the Twenty-First International Conference on Translating and the Computer, London.

Céline Beaudet. 1998. Littéracie et rédaction: vers la définition d'une pratique professionnelle. In G. A. Legault, editor, L'intervention : usages et méthodes. Éditions GGC, Sherbrooke, Canada, pages 68-88.

Lynne Bowker, and Elizabeth Marshman. 2011. Towards a Model of Active and Situated Learning in the Teaching of Computer-Aided Translation: Introducing the CERTT Project. In Journal of Translation Studies, 13-14. To appear.

Isabelle Clerc. 1998. L'enseignement de la rédaction professionnelle en milieu universitaire. In C. Préfontaine, L. Godard and G. Fortier, editors, Pour mieux comprendre la lecture et l'écriture : enseignement et apprentissage. Éditions Logiques, Montreal, pages 345-370.

[6] As a survey on LinguisTech users' satisfaction will be launched in March, 2012, we hope to have more information soon on that subject.

[7] Many resources are available for translation specialised tasks (see the list of translation and localization tools in Table 5).

Isabelle Clerc, et al. 2000. La démarche de rédaction. Éditions Nota bene, Quebec, Canada.

Paul Geoffrion. 1998. Le groupe de discussion. In B. Gauthier, editor, Recherche sociale: de la problématique à la collecte des données. Presses de l'Université du Québec, Québec, Canada, pages 303-328.

Éric Kavanagh. 1999. Analyse des fonctions d'un traitement de texte en regard des besoins du rédacteur professionnel. In Z. Guével and I. Clerc, editors, Les professions langagières à l'aube de l'an 2000. CIRAL, Quebec, Canada, pages 161-182.

Éric Kavanagh. 2006. La rédaction web : anatomie d'une « nouvelle » expertise. In A. Piolat, editor, Lire, écrire, communiquer et apprendre avec internet. Solal, Marseille, pages 175-201.

Alex Kuhn, Chris Quintana, and Elliot Soloway. 2009. Story Time : A New Way for Children to Write. In Proceedings of the 8th International Conference on Interaction Design and Children, pages 218-221, New York.

Päivi Majaranta, and Räihä Kari-Jouko. 2002. Twenty Years of Eye Typing: Systems and Design Issues. In Proceedings of the 2002 Symposium on Eye Tracking Research and Applications, pages 15-22, New York.

John Milton, and Vivying S. Y. Cheng. 2010. A Toolkit to Assist L2 Learners Become Independent Writers. In Proceedings of the NAACL HLT 2010 Workshop on Computational Linguistics and Writing: Writing Processes and Authoring Aids, pages 33-41, Stroudsburg, Pennsylvania.

Claude Morizio. 2006. La recherche d'information. Armand Colin, Paris.

Khédija Nakbi. 2002. La rédactologie : domaine, méthode et compétences. ASp, 37-38, pages 15-26. Retrieved December 7, 2011 from http://asp.revues.org/1428.

Author Index